FOSSIL FUELS

ENERGY: PAST, PRESENT, AND FUTURE | FOSSIL FUELS

EDITED BY ROBERT CURLEY, MANAGER, SCIENCE AND TECHNOLOGY

Britannica
Educational Publishing

IN ASSOCIATION WITH

ROSEN
EDUCATIONAL SERVICES

Published in 2012 by Britannica Educational Publishing
(a trademark of Encyclopædia Britannica, Inc.)
In association with Rosen Educational Services, LLC
29 East 21st Street, New York, NY 10010.

Distributed exclusively by Rosen Educational Services.
For a listing of additional Britannica Educational Publishing titles, call toll free (800) 237-9932.

First Edition

Britannica Educational Publishing
Michael I. Levy: Executive Editor
J.E. Luebering: Senior Manager
Marilyn L. Barton: Senior Coordinator, Production Control
Steven Bosco: Director, Editorial Technologies
Lisa S. Braucher: Senior Producer and Data Editor
Yvette Charboneau: Senior Copy Editor
Kathy Nakamura: Manager, Media Acquisition
Robert Curley: Manager, Science and Technology

Rosen Educational Services
Jeanne Nagle: Senior Editor
Nelson Sá: Art Director
Cindy Reiman: Photography Manager
Matthew Cauli: Designer, Cover Design
Introduction by Laura Loria

Library of Congress Cataloging-in-Publication Data

Fossil fuels/edited by Robert Curley.
   p. cm. — (Energy: past, present, and future)
"In association with Britannica Educational Publishing, Rosen Educational Services."
Includes bibliographical references and index.
ISBN 978-1-61530-491-2 (library binding)
1. Fossil fuels. I. Curley, Robert. II. Title. III. Series.
TP318.F67 2012
333.8'2—dc22

2010045687

Manufactured in the United States of America

Cover (front top, back) Derricks drilling for oil; (front bottom) A consumer pumping gas.
Shutterstock.com

Cover (front bottom) A consumer pumping gas. *Shutterstock.com*

On page x: Burning lumps of coal. Shutterstock.com

Pp. 1, 22, 46, 63, 81, 96, 110, 131, 133, 137 © www.istockphoto.com / Teun van den Dries

CONTENTS

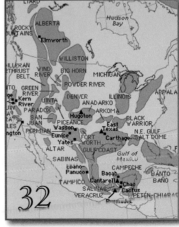

69

WILL BE HELD A

BERKELEY ARM

On TUESDAY Eve

At Six o'Clock

To consider the propriet

of Lighting the T

GA

WILLIAM

74

93

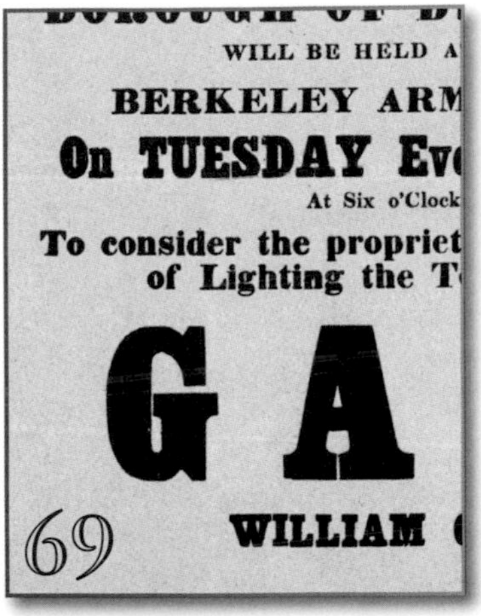

INTRODUCTION

Fossil fuels are of staggering significance throughout the world. Petroleum, natural gas, and coal are primary sources of energy that drive modern technology, affecting the lives of hundreds of millions of people. The production and sale of these fuels represent a billion-dollar-a-year industry, which greatly influences the global economy. Possession or, conversely, lack of these resources can sway the domestic and foreign policies of nations. Important resources such as these deserve careful consideration and in-depth analysis, which is the aim of this book. Within these pages lies a thorough analysis of the history, origins, production, and uses of fossil fuels.

As their collective name indicates, fossil fuels are formed from the preserved remains of plants and animals, and are buried deep underground. Petroleum is composed of carbon and hydrogen that has been passed through an organic phase in single-cell plants or planktonic animals, such as blue-green algae or foraminifera. The preserved remains of such organisms become petroleum through a process known as diagenesis. The first stage of diagenesis involves the conversion of the remains to kerogen. With pressure, heat, and time, the kerogen is converted to petroleum at depths of 750 to 4,800 metres (2,500 to 16,000 feet), commonly referred to as the oil window. The mature oil moves through the pores and capillaries of porous sedimentary rocks such as shale, either seeping to the surface or accumulating in reservoir beds, or traps. Petroleum is classified by its predominant hydrocarbon. There are five grades of crude oil based on specific gravity, ranging from heavy to light, the latter being the most desirable. Light products can be recovered from heavy oil, but at a considerable cost.

Oil is refined, or separated into different fractions and sometimes chemically altered in preparation for use, through three basic processes. In the first, known as separation, hydrocarbons of specific properties are separated from the crude oil through distillation, with the oil vapours produced by the heat being condensed at the top of a tower unit. Next, molecular conversion—for example, through the process of catalytic cracking—breaks down the molecules, creating the desired product in greater volume. Finally, the purification stage removes contaminants through one of several treatment processes.

After crude oil is refined, a variety of products can be manufactured. Gasoline is the most common product; others include diesel fuel, fuel oils, and gases such as propane, or liquid petroleum gas (LPG). Gasoline must meet three requirements. It must have an even combustion pattern, to prevent engine "knock," and allow the engine to start easily in cold weather. It also must meet changing environmental standards. Gasoline is graded with an octane rating, a number determined by taking the average score between two knock tests. The octane number, which for gasoline intended for automobiles ranges from 87 to 100, refers to the amount of octane that would be present in a fuel mixture whose performance matched the performance of the gasoline being tested in a knock engine. Gasoline contains a blend of up to 15 components with varying levels of volatility, to meet efficiency and environmental standards.

In the past, natural gas was erroneously considered merely a waste product of oil recovery processes. Both land plants and organic matter from the sea act as root material for the formation of natural gas. While petroleum is generated solely within the oil window, natural gas is much more pervasive; deposits are found above and below the oil window as well as within it. As with petroleum, natural gas migrates up from deep below Earth's surface and accumulates in traps.

Natural gas is classified according to its physical properties. Its principal components are the hydrocarbons methane and ethane, though it may contain others such as propane or butane. Nonhydrocarbon components include nitrogen, hydrogen, and carbon dioxide. Natural gas has three main properties: colour, odour, and flammability. Methane alone is colourless, odourless and highly flammable, but other gases influence these properties, even when present in minute amounts. Natural gas is measured in cubic metres at a pressure of 750 mm of mercury and a temperature of 15 °C (that is, at standard sea-level pressure and a temperature of 60 °F. The conditions under which it is measured are important due to the characteristics of gases, particularly expansion.

Coal is derived from plants that had originally grown in warm, humid climates. Today coal is found in a variety of temperate and even subarctic locations, a situation that can be explained through tectonic shifts and global climate changes over millions of years. Microorganisms interact with the organic matter to form peat, which is a coal precursor. The peat goes through chemical and physical changes on its way to becoming coal in a maturation process called coalification. The three factors that determine the maturity, and thus the quality, of coal are the same as those for petroleum and natural gas: time, pressure, and heat. Because it has been more greatly impacted by these three factors, coal that lies the deepest beneath Earth's surface is of highest quality.

Coal is ranked by its moisture content, volatility, mineral ash, fixed carbon content, and calorific value, or the amount of heat energy that is released when coal burned. The four ranks for coal, from lowest to highest, are lignite, subbituminous, bituminous, and anthracite. Bituminous coal is the most abundant. The most desirable coal has low moisture and volatility and high fixed carbon content and calorific value. Ash content determines the ways in which coal should be used. Coal is also typed by the organic substances it contains, called macerals. The three types are liptinite (algae or spores), vitrinite (wood), and inertinite (fossils). Coal can be combusted from its solid state or converted to a liquid or gas through varied processes.

Fossil fuels as an energy source are a relatively recent occurrence, but other uses of fossil fuels date back centuries. Early petroleum use can be traced back more than 5,000 years. Ancient Sumerians, Assyrians, and Babylonians exploited oil seeps, or petroleum that has naturally risen to the surface, for construction projects. Egyptians were the first known to use oil for medicinal purposes, and Persians used oil to create flammable weapons as early as 480 BCE. Oil became a precious commodity, as a machinery lubricant and a more efficient power source, during the Industrial Revolution. Acquiring more oil to fill this need necessitated better ways to tap petroleum deposits from deep underground. The first oil well was dug in 1859, by Edwin L. Drake in Pennsylvania. Drilling for oil became even more lucrative with the advent of automobile production in the early 20th century.

Natural gas was first used in Iran, sometime between 6000 and 2000 BCE. Also obtained via seeps, as petroleum was at first, the gas was first used by Iranians as a source of sacramental light. The Chinese were the first to drill for this particular energy source, in 211 BCE. Using primitive bits attached to bamboo poles, they reached depths of 150 metres (500 feet). Natural gas was discovered in England in the middle of the 17th century, but the British didn't start using the commodity widely until many years later. In America, natural gas was first distributed commercially in 1829 in the town of Fredonia, N.Y., where customers used it for lighting and cooking.

China was the world pioneer in the commercial use of coal, with distribution dating back to 1000 BCE. The Romans also were early users of coal, presumably dating back prior to 400 CE. Coal was mined in Western Europe beginning around 1200. Beginning in the 18th century, coal was used on a large scale in England. Cut off from British coal exports during the Revolutionary War, the American colonies began small mining operations of their own. The advent of rail travel, which relied upon coal to stoke locomotive engines, and the burgeoning industrial sector of the American economy throughout the 19th century spurred coal production in the United States.

Obtaining fossil fuels involves sophisticated machinery and geologic knowledge. When drilling for oil, a rotary drill connected to a drill pipe bores through the rock. As the hole is drilled, casing is added to prevent the transfer of fluid from the borehole to other areas. A structure called the derrick contains the machinery required to raise and lower the drill pipe to change the bit, which needs to be replaced frequently.

Variations of oil drilling include directional drilling, where the surface equipment is located at an angle away from the site, and offshore drilling, which employs platform rigs that may float or be anchored to the sea floor. When a well has been dug, it is finished off with production tubing, a more permanent casing for continuous production. Oil can then be recovered in three stages. In the primary stage, natural or artificial pressure causes the oil to rise to the surface. The secondary stage involves the injection of gas or water into the well to maintain or increase the pressure. Finally, tertiary recovery methods can be used; these involve the injection of natural gas or the application of heat.

Coal can be recovered through surface or underground mining. For surface mining, the process is straightforward.

The land is cleared of vegetation, and topsoil is retained for later replacement. The rock layer over the coal seam is drilled and blasted with explosives, and debris is removed. The coal deposit itself is drilled and blasted, and the loose coal is obtained and transported. Finally, the land is restored to a usable condition with the reserved topsoil.

Underground mining is subject to structural concerns. It begins with mine development, the creation of access points for workers and equipment. The room and pillar method carves out carefully spaced areas in the coal seam, or "rooms," which are separated by "pillars" of coal. During the creation of these rooms, up to 50 percent of the coal is recovered. Once this is accomplished, extraction from the pillars themselves begins, one row at a time, to allow for a safe collapse of the rooms. Longwall and shortwall mining removes coal in blocks, which are sheared mechanically or are undercut, blasted, and removed in varying lengths and thicknesses. Longwall mining often requires backfilling the mined areas with sand or waste materials, as collapse is too dangerous.

The supply of fossil fuels is determined by calculating both known and recoverable resources, combined with estimated undiscovered deposits. The world oil supply is estimated to be 2.39 trillion barrels, three-quarters of which consists of already known resources. Approximately 50,000 oil fields have been discovered since the middle of the 19th century, fewer than 40 of which are classified as supergiants—each of which is estimated to contain 5 billion barrels. Combined with the next rank, which is world-class giant fields, supergiants contain 80 percent of the world's known accessible oil. The top three oil producers are Saudi Arabia, the United States, and Russia. Fifteen oil-producing countries hold 93 percent of the world's oil reserves.

Compared to oil, natural gas deposits are a relatively underutilized resource. It is estimated that 45 percent of the world's recoverable gas has not yet been discovered. Its ultimate yield could rival that of oil, and is expected to last longer than oil is projected to, if use remains stable. The world endowment of natural gas is 344 trillion cubic metres, one-third of which is found in Russia. The United States has consumed one-half of its reserve to date, while Canada and Mexico have used only 17 percent and 11 percent of their resources, respectively, thus far.

The world coal supply is measured in two ways: proven resources, which are the estimated recoverable supply, and geological resources, meaning coal which cannot be recovered through current methods. Currently, it is estimated that the world's total proven resources will last for 300 to 500 years, although these figures depend on a stable rate of consumption. The United States, Russia, and China contain more than half of the world supply of proven reserves, with the U.S. leading with 27 percent of the total.

It remains to be seen whether fossil fuels will continue to meet the majority of the world's energy needs or if the use of renewable resources such as wind, water, or solar energy will eventually surpass petroleum, natural gas, and coal. Regardless, it must be acknowledged that the supply of these nonrenewable resources is finite, and therefore they should be used judiciously and wisely.

Petroleum is a complex mixture of hydrocarbons that occur in the Earth in liquid, gaseous, or solid forms. The term is often restricted to the liquid form, commonly called crude oil, though as a technical term it also includes natural gas and the viscous or solid form known as bitumen. The liquid and gaseous phases of petroleum constitute the most important of the primary fossil fuels. Indeed, liquid and gaseous hydrocarbons are so intimately associated in nature that it has become customary to shorten the expression "petroleum and natural gas" to "petroleum" when referring to both. The word *petroleum* (literally "rock oil," from the Latin *petra*, "rock" or "stone," and *oleum*, "oil") was first used in 1556 in a treatise published by the German mineralogist Georg Bauer, known as Georgius Agricola.

ORIGINS OF CRUDE OIL

Although it is recognized that the original source of carbon and hydrogen was in the materials that made up the primordial Earth, it is generally accepted that these two elements have had to pass through an organic phase to be combined into the varied complex molecules recognized as crude oil. This organic material has been subjected for hundreds of millions of years to extreme pressures and temperatures that have transformed it into the fuel source as it is known today.

From Planktonic Remains to Kerogen

The organic material that is the source of most oil has probably been derived from single-celled planktonic (free-floating) plants, such as diatoms and blue-green algae, and single-celled planktonic animals, such as foraminifera, which live in aquatic environments of marine, brackish, or fresh water. Such simple organisms are known to have been abundant long before the Paleozoic Era, which began some 542 million years ago.

Rapid burial of the remains of the single-celled planktonic plants and animals within fine-grained sediments effectively preserved them. This provided the organic materials, the so-called protopetroleum, for later diagenesis (i.e., the series of processes involving biological, chemical, and physical changes) into true petroleum.

The first, or immature, stage of petroleum formation is dominated by biological activity and chemical rearrangement, which convert organic matter to kerogen. This dark-coloured, insoluble product of bacterially altered plant and animal detritus is the source of most hydrocarbons generated in the later stages. During the first stage, biogenic methane is the only hydrocarbon generated in commercial quantities. The production of biogenic methane gas is part of the process of decomposition of organic matter carried out by anaerobic microorganisms (those capable of living in the absence of free oxygen).

From Kerogen to Petroleum

Deeper burial by continuing sedimentation, increasing temperatures, and advancing geologic age result in the mature stage of petroleum formation, during which the full range of petroleum compounds is produced from kerogen and other precursors by thermal degradation and cracking (the process by which heavy hydrocarbon molecules are broken up into lighter molecules). Depending on the amount and type of organic matter, oil generation occurs during the mature stage at depths of about 750 to 4,800 metres (2,500 to 16,000 feet) at temperatures between 65 and 150 °C (150 and 300 °F). This special environment is called the "oil window." In areas of higher than normal geothermal gradient (increase in temperature with depth), the oil window exists at shallower depths in younger sediments but is narrower. Maximum oil generation occurs from depths of 2,000 to 2,900 metres (6,600 to 9,500 feet). Below 2,900 metres primarily wet gas, a type of gas containing liquid hydrocarbons known as natural gas liquids, is formed.

Approximately 90 percent of the organic material in sedimentary source rocks is dispersed kerogen. Its composition varies, consisting as it does of a range of residual materials whose basic molecular structure takes the form of stacked sheets of aromatic hydrocarbon rings in which atoms of sulfur, oxygen, and nitrogen also occur. Attached to the ends of the rings are various hydrocarbon compounds, including normal paraffin chains. The mild heating of the kerogen in the oil window of a source rock over long periods of time results in the cracking of the kerogen molecules and the release of the attached paraffin chains. Further heating, perhaps assisted by the catalytic effect of clay minerals in the source rock matrix, may then produce soluble bitumen compounds, followed by the various saturated and unsaturated hydrocarbons, asphaltenes, and others of the thousands of hydrocarbon compounds that make up crude oil mixtures.

At the end of the mature stage, below about 4,800 metres (16,000 feet), depending on the geothermal gradient, kerogen becomes condensed in structure and chemically stable. In this environment, crude oil is no longer stable and the main hydrocarbon product is dry thermal methane gas.

ORIGIN IN SOURCE BEDS

Knowing the maximum temperature reached by a potential source rock during its geologic history helps in estimating the maturity of the organic material contained within it. Also, this information may indicate whether a region is gas-prone, oil-prone, both, or neither. The techniques employed to assess the maturity of potential source rocks in core samples include measuring the degree of darkening of fossil pollen grains and the colour changes in conodont fossils. In addition, geochemical evaluations can be made of mineralogical changes that were also induced by fluctuating paleotemperatures. In general, there appears to be a progressive evolution of crude oil characteristics from geologically younger, heavier, darker, more aromatic crudes to older, lighter, paler, more paraffinic types. There are, however, many exceptions to this rule, especially in regions with high geothermal gradients.

Accumulations of petroleum are usually found in relatively coarse-grained, permeable, and porous sedimentary reservoir rocks that contain little, if any, insoluble organic matter. It is unlikely that the vast quantities of oil now present in some reservoir rocks could have been generated from material of which no trace remains. Therefore, the site where commercial amounts of oil originated apparently is not always identical to the location at which they are ultimately discovered.

Oil is believed to have been generated in significant volumes only in fine-grained sedimentary rocks (usually clays, shales, or clastic carbonates) by geothermal action on kerogen, leaving an insoluble organic residue in the

Blocks of oil shale from a large deposit known as the Green River Formation, in the United States. U.S. Department of Energy/Photo Researchers, Inc.

source rock. The release of oil from the solid particles of kerogen and its movement in the narrow pores and capillaries of the source rock is termed primary migration.

Accumulating sediments can provide energy to the migration system. Primary migration may be initiated during compaction as a result of the pressure of overlying sediments. Continued burial causes clay to become dehydrated by the removal of water molecules that were loosely combined with the clay minerals. With increasing temperature, the newly generated hydrocarbons may become sufficiently mobile to leave the source beds in solution, suspension, or emulsion with the water being expelled from the compacting molecular lattices of the clay minerals. The hydrocarbon molecules would compose only a very small part of the migrating fluids, a few hundred parts per million.

MIGRATION THROUGH CARRIER BEDS

The hydrocarbons expelled from a source bed next move through the wider pores of carrier beds (e.g., sandstones or carbonates) that are coarser-grained and more permeable. This movement is termed secondary migration. The distinction between primary and secondary migration is based on pore size and rock type. In some cases, oil may migrate through such permeable carrier beds until it is trapped by a permeability barrier and forms an oil accumulation. In others, the oil may continue its migration until it becomes a seep on the surface of the Earth, where it will be broken down chemically by oxidation and bacterial action.

Since nearly all pores in subsurface sedimentary formations are water-saturated, the migration of oil takes place in an aqueous environment. Secondary migration may result from active water movement or can occur independently, either by displacement or by diffusion. Because the specific gravity of the water in the sedimentary formation is considerably higher than that of oil, the oil will float to the surface of the water in the course of geologic time and accumulate in the highest portion of a trap.

Accumulation in Reservoir Beds

The porosity (volume of pore spaces) and permeability (capacity for transmitting fluids) of carrier and reservoir beds are important factors in the migration and accumulation of oil. Most petroleum accumulations have been found in clastic reservoirs (sandstones and siltstones). Next in number are the carbonate reservoirs (limestones and dolomites). Accumulations of petroleum also occur in shales and igneous and metamorphic rocks because of porosity resulting from fracturing, but such reservoirs are relatively rare. Porosities in reservoir rocks usually range from about 5 to 30 percent, but all available pore space is not occupied by petroleum. A certain amount of residual formation water cannot be displaced and is always present.

Reservoir rocks may be divided into two main types: (1) those in which the porosity and permeability is primary, or inherent, and (2) those in which they are secondary, or induced. Primary porosity and permeability are dependent on the size, shape, and grading and packing of the sediment grains and also on the manner of their initial consolidation. Secondary porosity and permeability result from post-depositional factors, such as solution, recrystallization, fracturing, weathering during temporary exposure at the Earth's surface, and further cementation. These secondary factors may either enhance or diminish the inherent conditions.

OIL TRAPS

After secondary migration in carrier beds, oil finally collects in a trap. The fundamental characteristic of a trap is an upward convex form of porous and permeable reservoir rock that is sealed above by a denser, relatively impermeable cap rock (e.g., shale or evaporites). The trap may be of any shape, the critical factor being that it is a closed, inverted container. A rare exception is hydrodynamic trapping, in which high water saturation of low-permeability sediments reduces hydrocarbon permeability to near zero, resulting in a water block and an accumulation of petroleum down the structural dip of a sedimentary bed below the water in the sedimentary formation.

STRUCTURAL TRAPS

Traps can be formed in many ways. Those formed by tectonic events, such as folding or faulting of rock units, are called structural traps. The most common structural traps are anticlines, upfolds of strata that appear as ovals on the horizontal planes of geologic maps. About 80 percent of the world's petroleum has been found in anticlinal traps. Most anticlines were produced by lateral pressure, but some have resulted from the draping and subsequent

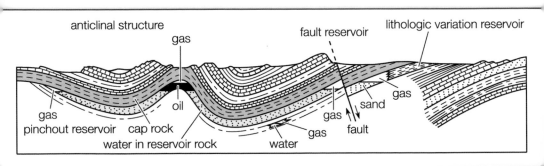

Principal types of traps. Encyclopædia Britannica, Inc.

compaction of accumulating sediments over topographic highs. The closure of an anticline is the vertical distance between its highest point and the spill plane, the level at which the petroleum can escape if the trap is filled beyond capacity. Some traps are filled with petroleum to their spill plane, but others contain considerably smaller amounts than they can accommodate on the basis of their size.

Another kind of structural trap is the fault trap. Here, rock fracture results in a relative displacement of strata that forms a barrier to petroleum migration. A barrier can occur when an impermeable bed is brought into contact with a carrier bed. Sometimes the faults themselves provide a seal against "updip" migration when they contain impervious clay gouge material between their walls. Faults and folds often combine to produce traps, each providing a part of the container for the enclosed petroleum. Faults can, however, allow the escape of petroleum from a former trap if they breach the cap rock seal.

Other structural traps are associated with salt domes. Such traps are formed by the upward movement of salt masses from deeply buried evaporite beds, and they occur along the folded or faulted flanks of the salt plug or on top of the plug in the overlying folded or draped sediments.

STRATIGRAPHIC TRAPS

A second major class of oil traps is the stratigraphic trap. It is related to sediment deposition or erosion and is bounded on one or more sides by zones of low permeability. Because tectonics ultimately control deposition and erosion, however, few stratigraphic traps are completely without structural influence. The geologic history of most sedimentary basins contains the prerequisites for the formation of stratigraphic traps. Typical examples are fossil carbonate reefs, marine sandstone bars, and deltaic distributary channel sandstones. When buried, each of these geomorphic features provides a potential reservoir, which is often surrounded by finer-grained sediments that may act as source or cap rocks.

Sediments eroded from a landmass and deposited in an adjacent sea change from coarse- to fine-grained with increasing depth of water and distance from shore. Permeable sediments thus grade into impermeable sediments, forming a permeability barrier that eventually could trap migrating petroleum.

There are many other types of stratigraphic traps. Some are associated with the many transgressions and regressions of the sea that have occurred over geologic time and the resulting deposits of differing porosities. Others are caused by processes that increase secondary porosity, such as the dolomitization of limestones or the weathering of strata once located at the Earth's surface.

HISTORY OF USE

On a time scale within the span of prospective human history, the utilization of oil as a major source of energy will doubtless be seen as a transitory affair. Nonetheless, it will have been an affair of profound importance to world industrialization.

EXPLOITATION OF SURFACE SEEPS

The use of petroleum for purposes other than energy dates far back in history. Small surface occurrences of petroleum in the form of natural gas and oil seeps have been known from early times. The ancient Sumerians, Assyrians, and Babylonians used crude oil and asphalt ("pitch") collected from large seeps at Tuttul (modern-day Hīt in Iraq) on the Euphrates for many purposes more than 5,000 years

Persian warriors were known to use oil-soaked flaming arrows in battle, as shown in this depiction of the Battle of Salamis. Private Collection/© Look and Learn/The Bridgeman Art Library

ago. Liquid oil was first used as a medicine by the ancient Egyptians, presumably as a wound dressing, liniment, and laxative.

Oil products were valued as weapons of war in the ancient world. The Persians used incendiary arrows wrapped in oil-soaked fibres at the siege of Athens in 480 BCE. Early in the Christian era the Arabs and Persians distilled crude oil to obtain flammable products for military purposes. Probably as a result of the Arab invasion of Spain, the industrial art of distillation into illuminants became available in western Europe by the 12th century.

Several centuries later, Spanish explorers discovered oil seeps in present-day Cuba, Mexico, Bolivia, and Peru. In North America oil seeps were plentiful and were noted by early explorers in what are now New York and

Pennsylvania, where Native Americans were reported to have used the oil for medicinal purposes.

EXTRACTION FROM UNDERGROUND RESERVOIRS

Until the beginning of the 19th century, illumination in the United States and in many other countries was little improved over that known by the early Greeks and Romans. The need for better illumination that accompanied the increasing development of urban centres made it necessary to search for new sources of oil, especially since whales, which had long provided fuel for lamps, were becoming harder and harder to find. By the mid-19th century kerosene, or coal oil, derived from coal was in common use in both North America and Europe.

Edwin Drake (right, foreground) *at the site of his first well in Titusville, Pa.*
Hulton Archive/Getty Images

The Industrial Revolution brought on an ever-growing demand for a cheaper and more convenient source of lubricants as well as illuminating oil. It also required better sources of energy. Energy had previously been provided by human and animal muscle and later by the combustion of such solid fuels as wood, peat, and coal. These were collected with considerable effort and laboriously transported to the site where the energy source was needed. Liquid petroleum, on the other hand, was a more easily transportable source of energy. Oil was a much more concentrated and flexible form of fuel than anything previously available.

The stage was set for the first well specifically drilled for oil, a project undertaken by Edwin L. Drake in northwestern Pennsylvania. The completion of the well in August 1859 established the groundwork for the petroleum industry and ushered in the closely associated modern industrial age. Within a short time inexpensive oil from underground reservoirs was being processed at already existing coal-oil refineries, and by the end of the century oil fields had been discovered in 14 states from New York to California and from Wyoming to Texas. During the same period, oil fields were found in Europe and East Asia as well.

PETROLEUM FUEL PRODUCTS

Although petroleum is the source material for many chemicals and synthetic materials such as plastic, its most important use is as a fuel. Following are some of the most prominent petroleum fuel products.

GASES

Gaseous refinery products include hydrogen, fuel gas, ethane, and propane or LPG. Most of the hydrogen is

EDWIN L. DRAKE

(b. March 29, 1819, Greenville, N.Y., U.S.—d. Nov. 8, 1880, Bethlehem, Pa.)

Edwin Laurentine Drake drilled the first productive oil well in the United States.

A railway conductor in New Haven, Conn., Drake bought a small amount of stock in the Pennsylvania Rock Oil Company, which gathered oil from ground-level seepages at Titusville, Pa., for medicinal uses. In Titusville on business, Drake studied the techniques of drilling salt wells. With the encouragement of George H. Bissell, a local landowner who was aware of the younger Benjamin Silliman's report of the potential value of petroleum, Drake persuaded the company to lease its land for drilling operations. He began drilling in 1858 and struck oil at a depth of 21 metres (69 feet) on Aug. 27, 1859.

With the spread of Drake's drilling techniques, Titusville and other northwestern Pennsylvania communities became boom towns. Drake failed to patent his drilling methods, however, and later lost his money in oil speculation. After 10 years of poverty, he was finally pensioned by the Pennsylvania legislature.

consumed in refinery desulfurization facilities; small quantities may be delivered to the refinery fuel system. Refinery fuel gas usually has a heating value similar to natural gas and is consumed in plant operations. Periodic variability in heating value makes it unsuitable for delivery to consumer gas systems. Ethane may be recovered from the refinery fuel system for use as a petrochemical feedstock. Liquefied petroleum gas, or LPG, is a convenient, portable fuel for domestic heating and cooking or light industrial use.

GASOLINE

Motor gasoline, or petrol, must meet three primary requirements. It must provide an even combustion pattern, start easily in cold weather, and meet prevailing environmental requirements.

OCTANE RATING

In order to meet the first requirement, gasoline must burn smoothly in the engine without premature detonation, or knocking. Severe knocking can dissipate power output and even cause damage to the engine. When gasoline engines became more powerful in the 1920s, it was discovered that some fuels knocked more readily than others. Experimental studies led to the determination that, of the standard fuels available at the time, the most extreme knock was produced by a fuel composed of pure normal heptane, while the least knock was produced by pure isooctane. This discovery led to the development of the octane scale for defining gasoline quality. Thus, when a motor gasoline gives the same performance in a standard knock engine as a mixture of 90 percent isooctane and 10 percent normal heptane, it is given an octane rating of 90.

There are two methods for carrying out the knock engine test. Research octane is measured under mild conditions of temperature and engine speed (49 °C [120 °F] and 600 revolutions per minute, or RPM), while motor octane is measured under more severe conditions (149 °C [300 °F] and 900 RPM). For many years the research octane number was found to be the more accurate measure of engine performance and was usually quoted alone. After the advent of unleaded fuels in the mid-1970s, however, motor octane measurements were frequently found to limit actual engine performance. As a result the road

TETRAETHYL LEAD

Tetraethyl lead is an organometallic compound that at one time was the chief antiknock agent for automotive fuels. Manufactured by the action of ethyl chloride on a powdered alloy of lead and sodium, the compound is a dense, colourless liquid that is quite volatile, boiling at about 200 °C (400 °F). As an antidetonant (i.e., antiknock agent), tetraethyl lead was added to gasoline in quantities not exceeding 3 cubic cm (0.2 cubic inch) per gallon; a small quantity of ethylene dibromide and sometimes ethylene dichloride was added to prevent accumulation of lead deposits in the engine. Tetraethyl lead can cause acute or chronic lead poisoning if inhaled or absorbed through the skin. Its use declined markedly during the 1970s because the products of its combustion are toxic and detrimental to catalytic devices that were introduced to nullify other pollutants emitted in the exhaust gases of engines.

octane number, which is a simple average of the research and motor values, became most frequently used to define fuel quality. Automotive gasolines generally range from research octane number 87 to 100, while gasoline for piston-engine aircraft ranges from research octane number 115 to 130.

Each naphtha component that is blended into gasoline is tested separately for its octane rating. Reformate, alkylate, polymer, and cracked naphtha, as well as butane, all rank high (90 or higher) on this scale, while straight-run naphtha may rank at 70 or less. In the 1920s it was discovered that the addition of tetraethyl lead would substantially enhance the octane rating of various naphthas. Each naphtha component was found to have a unique response to lead additives, some combinations being found to be synergistic and others antagonistic. This

GASOLINE BLENDING

One of the most critical economic issues for a petroleum refiner is selecting the optimal combination of components to produce final gasoline products. Gasoline blending is much more complicated than a simple mixing of components. First, a typical refinery may have as many as eight to 15 different hydrocarbon streams to consider as blend stocks. These may range from butane, the most volatile component, to a heavy naphtha and include several gasoline naphthas from crude distillation, catalytic cracking, and thermal processing units in addition to alkylate, polymer, and reformate. Modern gasoline may be blended to meet simultaneously 10 to 15 different quality specifications, such as vapour pressure; initial, intermediate, and final boiling points; sulfur content; colour; stability; aromatics content; olefin content; octane measurements for several different portions of the blend; and other local governmental or market restrictions. Since each of the individual components contributes uniquely in each of these quality areas and each bears a different cost of manufacture, the proper allocation of each component into its optimal disposition is of major economic importance.

In order to address this problem, most refiners employ linear programming, a mathematical technique that permits the rapid selection of an optimal solution from a multiplicity of feasible alternative solutions. Each component is characterized by its specific properties and cost of manufacture, and each gasoline grade requirement is similarly defined by quality requirements and relative market value. The linear programming solution specifies the unique disposition of each component to achieve maximum operating profit. The next step is to measure carefully the rate of addition of each component to the blend and collect it in storage tanks for final inspection before delivering it for sale. Still, the problem is not fully resolved until the product is actually delivered into customers' tanks. Frequently, last-minute changes in shipping schedules or production qualities require the reblending of finished gasolines or the substitution of a high-quality (and therefore costlier) grade for one of more immediate demand even though it may generate less income for the refinery.

gave rise to very sophisticated techniques for designing the optimal blends of available components into desired grades of gasoline.

The advent of leaded, or ethyl, gasoline led to the manufacture of high-octane fuels and became universally employed throughout the world after World War II. Lead is still an essential component of high-octane aviation gasoline, but, beginning in 1975, environmental legislation in the United States restricted the use of lead additives in automotive gasoline. Similar restrictions have since been adopted in most developed countries. The required use of lead-free gasoline placed a premium on the construction of new catalytic reformers and alkylation units for increasing yields of high-octane gasoline ingredients and on the exclusion of low-octane naphthas from the gasoline blend.

High-Volatile and Low-Volatile Components

The second major criterion for gasoline—that the fuel be sufficiently volatile to enable the car engine to start quickly in cold weather—is accomplished by the addition of butane, a very low-boiling paraffin, to the gasoline blend. Fortunately, butane is also a high-octane component with little alternate economic use, so its application has historically been maximized in gasoline.

Another requirement, that a quality gasoline have a high energy content, has traditionally been satisfied by including higher-boiling components in the blend. However, both of these practices are now called into question on environmental grounds. The same high volatility that provides good starting characteristics in cold weather can lead to high evaporative losses of gasoline during refueling operations, and the inclusion of high-boiling components to increase the energy content of the gasoline can also increase the emission of unburned hydrocarbons from engines on start-up. As a result, since 1990, gasoline

Workers install a diesel engine at a Mercedes assembly plant in Germany. Diesel engines use compression, rather than a spark, to ignite fuel. Peter Ginter/Science Faction/Getty Images

consumed in the United States has been reformulated to meet stringent new environmental standards. Among these changes are the inclusion of some oxygenated compounds (methyl or ethyl alcohol or methyl tertiary butyl ether [MTBE]) in order to reduce the emission of carbon monoxide and nitrogen oxides.

DIESEL FUEL

The fuel for diesel engines is ordinarily obtained from crude oil after the more volatile portions used in gasoline are removed. Diesel fuel is typically cheaper than gasoline because it requires less refining, and its ignition point is much higher. In diesel engines the fuel is ignited not by a spark, as in gasoline engines, but by the heat of air compressed in the cylinder, with the fuel injected in a spray into the hot compressed air.

Several grades of diesel fuel are manufactured—for example, "light-middle" and "middle" distillates for high-speed engines with frequent and wide variations in load and speed (such as trucks and automobiles) and "heavy" distillates for low- and medium-speed engines with sustained loads and speeds (such as stationary engines). Performance criteria are cetane number (a measure of ease of ignition), ease of volatilization, and sulfur content. The highest grades, for automobile and truck engines, are the most volatile, while the lowest grades, for low-speed engines, are the least volatile, leave the most carbon residue, and commonly have the highest sulfur content.

Sulfur is a critical polluting component of diesel and has been the object of much regulation. Traditional "regular" grades of diesel fuel contained as much as 5,000 parts per million (ppm) by weight sulfur. In the 1990s "low sulfur" grades containing up to 500 ppm sulfur were introduced, and in the 2000s "ultra-low sulfur" (ULSD) grades containing a maximum of 15 ppm were made standard. So-called "zero-sulfur," or "sulfur-free," diesels containing no more than 10 ppm are also available. Lower sulfur content reduces emissions of sulfur compounds implicated in acid rain and allows diesel vehicles to be equipped with highly effective emission-control systems that would otherwise be damaged by higher concentrations of sulfur.

Fuel Oil

Furnace oil consists largely of residues from crude oil refining. These are blended with other suitable gas oil fractions in order to achieve the viscosity required for convenient handling. As a residue product, fuel oil is the only refined product of significant quantity that commands a market price lower than the cost of crude oil.

Because the sulfur contained in the crude oil is concentrated in the residue material, fuel oil sulfur levels naturally vary from less than 1 to as much as 6 percent. The sulfur level is not critical to the combustion process as long as the flue gases do not impinge on cool surfaces (which could lead to corrosion by the condensation of acidic sulfur trioxide). However, residual fuels may contain large quantities of heavy metals such as nickel and vanadium; these produce ash upon burning and can foul burner systems. Such contaminants are not easily removed and usually lead to lower market prices for fuel oils with high metal contents.

In order to reduce air pollution, most industrialized countries now restrict the sulfur content of fuel oils. Such regulation has led to the construction of residual desulfurization units or cokers in refineries that produce these fuels.

SIGNIFICANCE OF OIL IN MODERN TIMES

The significance of oil as a world energy source is difficult to overdramatize. The growth in energy production that has taken place since the early 20th century is unprecedented, and increasing oil production has been by far the major contributor to that growth. Every day an immense and intricate system moves millions of barrels of oil from producers to consumers. The production and consumption of oil is of vital importance to international relations and has frequently been a decisive factor in the determination of foreign policy. The position of a country in this system depends on its production capacity as related to its consumption. The possession of oil deposits is sometimes the determining factor between a rich and a poor country. For any country, however, the presence or absence of oil has a major economic consequence.

CHAPTER 2
OBTAINING
PETROLEUM

After petroleum has formed underground, a great technological and human effort must be made before it is used in daily life. Workers must find the substance at its most accessible points, which can be anywhere on the planet, and then extract it from below Earth's surface.

WORLD DISTRIBUTION OF PETROLEUM

Petroleum is not distributed evenly around the world. More than half of the world's proven oil reserves are located in the Middle East (including Iran but not North Africa)— that is to say, the Middle East contains more oil than the rest of the world combined. Following the Middle East are Canada and the United States, Latin America, Africa, and the region occupied by the former Soviet Union. Each of these regions contains less than 15 percent of the world's proven reserves.

The amount of oil a given region produces is not always proportionate to the size of its proven reserves. For example, the Middle East contains more than 50 percent of the world's proven reserves but accounts for only about 30 percent of global oil production (though this figure is still higher than in any other region). The United States, by contrast, lays claim to only about 1.5 percent of the world's proven reserves but produces about 10 percent of the world's oil.

OIL FIELDS

Two overriding principles apply to world petroleum production. First, most petroleum is contained in a few large fields, but most fields are small. Second, as exploration progresses, the average size of the fields discovered decreases, as does the amount of petroleum found per

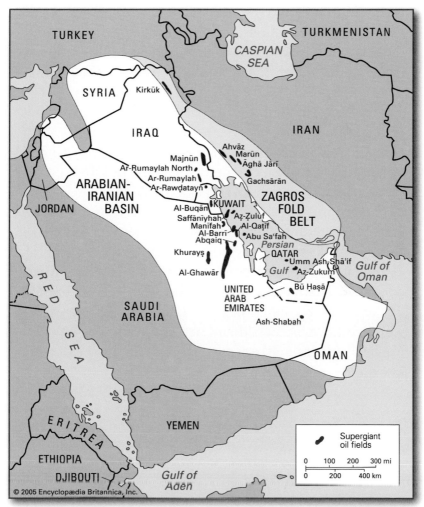

Major oil fields of the Arabian-Iranian basin region. Encyclopædia Britannica, Inc.

unit of exploratory drilling. In any region, the large fields are usually discovered first.

Since exploration for oil began during the early 1860s, some 50,000 oil fields have been discovered. More than 90 percent of these fields are insignificant in their impact on world oil production. The two largest classes of fields are the supergiants, fields with 5 billion or more barrels of ultimately recoverable oil, and world-class giants, fields with 500 million to 5 billion barrels of ultimately recoverable oil. Fewer than 40 supergiant oil fields have been found worldwide, yet these fields originally contained about one-half of all the oil so far discovered. The Arabian-Iranian sedimentary basin in the Persian Gulf region contains two-thirds of these supergiant fields. Of the remaining supergiants, there are two in the United States, two in Russia, two in Mexico, one in Libya, one in Algeria, one in Venezuela, and two in China.

The nearly 280 world-class giant fields thus far discovered, plus the supergiants, account for about 80 percent of the world's known recoverable oil. There are, in addition, approximately 1,000 known large oil fields that initially contained between 50 million and 500 million barrels. These fields account for some 14 to 16 percent of the world's known oil. Less than 5 percent of the known fields originally contained roughly 95 percent of the world's known oil.

SEDIMENTARY BASINS

Giant petroleum fields and significant petroleum-producing sedimentary basins are closely associated. In some basins, huge amounts of petroleum apparently have been generated because perhaps only about 10 percent of the generated petroleum is trapped and preserved.

The Arabian-Iranian sedimentary basin is predominant because it contains more than 20 supergiant fields. No other basin has more than one such field. In 20 of the 26 most significant oil-containing basins, the 10 largest fields originally contained more than 50 percent of the known recoverable oil. Known world oil reserves are concentrated in a relatively small number of giant fields in a few sedimentary basins.

Worldwide, approximately 600 sedimentary basins are known to exist. About 160 of these have yielded oil, but only 26 are significant producers and seven of these account for more than 65 percent of total known oil. Exploration has occurred in another 240 basins, but discoveries of commercial significance have not been made.

GEOLOGIC STUDY AND EXPLORATION

Current geologic understanding can usually distinguish between geologically favourable and unfavourable conditions for oil accumulation early in the exploration cycle. Thus, only a relatively few exploratory wells may be necessary to indicate whether a region is likely to contain significant amounts of oil. Modern petroleum exploration is an efficient process. If giant fields exist, it is likely that most of the oil in a region will be found by the first 50 to 250 exploratory wells. This number may be exceeded if there is a much greater than normal amount of major prospects or if exploration drilling patterns are dictated by either political or unusual technological considerations. Thus, while undiscovered commercial oil fields may exist in some of the 240 explored but seemingly barren basins, it is unlikely that they will be of major importance since the largest are normally found early in the exploration process.

TAR SANDS

Tar sands are deposits of loose sand or partially consolidated sandstone that are saturated with highly viscous bitumen, a solid or semisolid form of petroleum. Oil recovered from tar sands is commonly referred to as synthetic crude and is a potentially significant form of fossil fuel.

Deposits of bitumen, like those of other heavy hydrocarbons, are thought to be degraded remnants of accumulations of conventional (light-to-medium) oil. Degradation occurs when conventional oil migrates toward the surface and encounters, at temperatures below 93 °C (200 °F), descending rainwater containing oxygen and bacteria. This leads to the formation of a tarlike substance at the oil and water contact that eventually invades the entire oil pool. The lighter crude-oil fractions are removed by solution, while the paraffins are removed by the bacteria in the water.

Open-pit techniques can be used to mine thick deposits of tar sands when they occur near the surface. After the tar sand has been excavated, the bitumen has to be separated from the sand and then concentrated and cleaned. This crude bitumen is upgraded in a special coking unit, which produces a blend of lighter hydrocarbon fractions to yield synthetic crude, naphtha, kerosene, and gas oil. Deeper deposits are extracted by so-called in situ methods, in which steam is injected into the deposits to liquefy the bitumen, which flows closer to the surface where it can be pumped out.

The largest known deposits of tar sands occur in the Athabasca River valley of Alberta, Canada. The world's largest commercial projects for synthetic oil production from tar sands are being carried out in the Athabasca region. Synthetic crude represents approximately half of Canada's total liquid petroleum production.

The remaining 200 basins have had little or no exploration, but they have had sufficient geologic study to indicate their dimensions, amount and type of sediments, and general structural character. Most of the underexplored (or frontier) basins are located in difficult environments, such as polar regions or submerged continental margins. The larger sedimentary basins—those containing more than 833,000 cubic km (200,000 cubic miles) of sediments—account for some 70 percent of known world petroleum. Future exploration will have to involve the smaller basins as well as the more expensive and difficult frontier basins.

Status of the World Oil Supply

On several occasions in recent history—most notably, during the oil crises of 1973–74 and 1978–79 and during the first half of 2008—the price of petroleum has risen steeply. Because oil is such a crucial source of energy worldwide, these rapid rises in price spark recurrent debates about the accessibility of global supplies, the extent to which producers will be able to meet demand in decades to come, and the potential for alternative sources of energy to mitigate concerns about energy supply.

How much oil does Earth have? The short answer to this question is, "Nobody knows." In its 2000 assessment of total world oil supplies, the U.S. Geological Survey (USGS) estimated that about 3 trillion barrels of recoverable oil originally existed on Earth and that about 710 billion barrels of that amount had been consumed by 1995. The survey acknowledged, however, that the total recoverable amount of oil could be higher or lower—3 trillion barrels was not a guess but an average of estimates based on different probabilities. This caveat notwithstanding, the USGS estimate was hotly disputed. Some experts said

that technological improvements would create a situation
in which much more oil would be ultimately recoverable,
whereas others said that much less oil would be recoverable and that more than one-half of the world's original oil
supply had already been consumed.

There is ambiguity in all such predictions. When
industry experts speak of total "global oil reserves," they
refer specifically to the amount of oil that is thought to
be recoverable, not the total amount remaining on Earth.
What is counted as "recoverable," however, varies from
estimate to estimate. Analysts make distinctions between
"proven reserves"—those that can be demonstrated as
recoverable with reasonable certainty, given existing economic and technological conditions—and reserves that
may be recoverable but are more speculative. The *Oil &
Gas Journal*, a prominent weekly magazine for the petroleum industry, estimated in late 2007 that the world's
proven reserves amounted to roughly 1.3 trillion barrels.
To put this number in context, the world's population consumed about 30 billion barrels of oil in 2007. At this rate
of consumption, disregarding any new reserves that might
be found, the world's proven reserves would be depleted
in about 43 years.

By any estimation, it is clear that Earth has a finite
amount of oil and that global demand is expected to
increase. In 2007 the National Petroleum Council, an advi-
sory committee to the U.S. secretary of energy, projected
that world demand for oil would rise from 86 million barrels per day to as much as 138 million barrels per day in
2030. Yet experts remain divided on whether the world
will be able to supply so much oil.

Some argue that the world has reached "peak oil"—its
peak rate of oil production. The "peak-oil theory" suggests
that once global peak oil has been reached, the rate of oil

production in the world will progressively decline, with severe economic consequences to oil-importing countries. The controversial theory draws on studies that show how production from individual oil fields and from oil-producing regions has tended to increase to a point in time and then decrease thereafter. For example, oil production in the continental United States increased steadily through the early and mid-20th century until it peaked in 1970. By 2008 it had declined by almost 50 percent from its peak.

A more widely accepted view is that, through the early 21st century at least, production capacity will not be limited by the amount of oil in the ground but by other factors, such as geopolitics or economics. One concern is that growing dominance by nationalized oil companies, as opposed to independent oil firms, can lead to a situation in which countries with access to oil reserves will limit production for political or economic gain. A separate concern is that nonconventional sources of oil—such as tar-sand reserves, oil-shale deposits, or reserves that are found under very deep water—will be significantly more expensive to produce than conventional crude oil unless new technologies are developed that reduce production costs.

Major Oil-Producing Countries

As is mentioned earlier, petroleum resources are not distributed evenly around the world. Indeed, according to estimates published for 2006 by the U.S. Department of Energy, as few as 15 countries account for 75 percent of the world's oil production and hold 93 percent of its reserves. Significantly, these countries are projected to have a correspondingly large percentage of the world's remaining undiscovered oil resources.

Saudi Arabia has the largest proven oil reserves of any country—some 260 billion barrels, or approximately 20 percent of the world's proven reserves—not to mention significant potential for additional discoveries. The discovery that transformed Saudi Arabia into a leading oil country was the Al-Ghawār field. Discovered in 1948, this field has proved to be the world's largest, containing an estimated 70 billion barrels after 60 years of production. Another important discovery was the Saffānīyah offshore field in the Persian Gulf. It is the third largest oil field in the world and the largest offshore. Saudi Arabia has eight other supergiant oil fields. Saudi fields, as well as many other Middle Eastern fields, are located in the great Arabian-Iranian basin.

Russia is thought to possess excellent potential for new discoveries. It has significant proven reserves—some

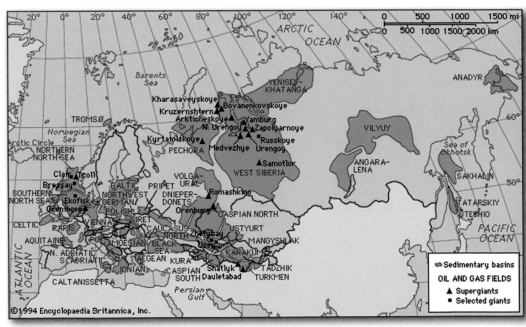

Sedimentary basins and major oil and gas fields of Europe, Russia, Transcaucasia, and Central Asia. Encyclopædia Britannica, Inc.

60 billion barrels, or almost 5 percent of the world total—and is the world's leading petroleum producer. Russian oil is derived from many sedimentary basins within the vast country, in which two supergiant fields, Samotlor and Romashkino, were discovered in 1964 and 1949, respectively. Production from these mature fields is on the decline, however, so that total Russian oil output is maintained by production at new fields. The best prospects for new Russian discoveries appear to exist in the difficult and expensive frontier areas such as Sakhalin Island.

North America also has many sedimentary basins. Basins in the United States have been intensively explored and their oil resources developed. More than 33,000 oil fields have been found, but only two are supergiants (Prudhoe Bay in the North Slope region of Alaska and East Texas). Cumulatively, the United States has produced more oil than any other country. Its proven oil reserves amount to some 20 billion barrels, representing less than 2 percent of the world total, but it is still considered to have significant remaining undiscovered oil resources. Prudhoe Bay, which accounted for approximately 17 percent of U.S. oil production during the mid-1980s, is in decline. This situation, coupled with declining oil production in the conterminous United States, has contributed to a significant drop in domestic oil output.

Mexico has more than 10 billion barrels of proven oil reserves and is one of the top 10 oil producers in the world. However, its principal supergiant oil field (Cantarell, offshore of Campeche state) is in decline, making it difficult to sustain current production levels well into the 21st century.

Canada has less than 10 billion barrels of proven reserves of conventional liquid oil, but huge deposits of oil sands in the Athabasca region of western Canada bring

Sedimentary basins and major oil and gas fields of North America.
Encyclopædia Britannica, Inc.

the country's total proven oil reserves to approximately
175 billion barrels, second only to oil giant Saudi Arabia.
Canada's largest oil field is Hibernia, discovered in the
Jeanne d'Arc Basin off Newfoundland in 1979. This giant
field began producing in 1997 and was soon joined by two
other fields, Terra Nova (first production 2002) and White
Rose (first production 2005).

The Middle Eastern countries of Iraq, Kuwait, and
Iran are each estimated to have proven oil reserves in
excess of 100 billion barrels. Together they account for
more than 25 percent of all proven reserves in the world.

These countries have a number of supergiant fields, all of which are located in the Arabian-Iranian basin, including Kuwait's Al-Burqān field. Al-Burqān is the world's second largest oil field, having originally contained 75 billion barrels of recoverable oil. Iraq possesses a significant potential for additional oil discoveries.

DRILLING FOR OIL

Drilling engineering was among the first applications of technology to oil-field practices in the early 20th century. Today the drilling engineer is responsible for the design of the earth-penetration techniques, the selection of casing and safety equipment, and, often, the direction of the operations. These functions involve understanding the nature of the rocks to be penetrated, the stresses in these rocks, and the techniques available to drill into and control the underground reservoirs. Modern drilling involves organizing a vast array of machinery and materials, investing huge funds, and acknowledging the safety and welfare of the general public.

CABLE TOOLING

Early oil wells were drilled with impact-type tools in a method called cable-tool drilling. A weighted, chisel-shaped bit was suspended from a cable to a lever at the surface, where an up-and-down motion of the lever caused the bit to chip away the rock at the bottom of the hole. The drilling had to be halted periodically to allow loose rock chips and liquids to be removed with a collecting device attached to the cable. At these times the chipping tip of the bit was sharpened, or "dressed" by the tool dresser. The borehole had to be free of liquids during the drilling so that the bit could remove rock effectively. This dry condition of the hole allowed oil and gas to flow to the surface when the bit penetrated a producing formation, thus creating the image of a "gusher" as a successful oil well. Often a large amount of oil was wasted before the well could be capped and brought under control.

THE ROTARY DRILL

During the middle and late 20th century, rotary drilling became the preferred penetration method for oil and gas wells. In this method a special tool, the drill bit, rotates while bearing down on the bottom of the well, thus gouging and chipping its way downward. Probably the greatest advantage of rotary drilling over cable tooling is that the well bore is kept full of liquid during drilling. A weighted fluid (drilling mud) is circulated through the well bore to serve two important purposes. By its hydrostatic pressure, it prevents the entry of the formation fluids into the well, thereby preventing "blowouts" and gushers. In addition, the drilling mud carries the crushed rock to the surface, so that drilling is continuous until the bit wears out.

Rotary drilling techniques have enabled wells to be drilled to depths of more than 9,000 metres. Formations having fluid pressures greater than 1,400 kilograms per square centimetre (20,000 pounds per square inch) and temperatures greater than 250° C (480° F) have been successfully penetrated.

THE DRILL PIPE

The drill bit is connected to the surface equipment through the drill pipe, a heavy-walled tube through which the drilling mud is fed to the bottom of the borehole. In most cases, the drill pipe also transmits the rotary motion to the bit from a turntable at the surface. The top piece of the drill pipe is a tube of square (or occasionally six- or eight-sided) cross section called the kelly. The kelly passes through a similarly shaped hole in the turntable. At the bottom end of the drill pipe are extra-heavy sections called drill collars, which serve to concentrate the weight on the rotating bit. In order to help maintain a vertical well bore, the drill pipe above the collars is usually kept in tension.

The drilling mud leaves the drill pipe through the bit in such a way that it scours the loose rock from the bottom and carries it to the surface. Drilling mud is carefully formulated to assure the correct weight and viscosity properties for the required tasks. After screening to remove the rock chips, the mud is held in open pits or metal tanks to be recirculated through the well. The mud is picked up by piston pumps and forced through a swivel joint at the top of the kelly.

THE DERRICK

The hoisting equipment that is used to raise and lower the drill pipe, along with the machinery for rotating the pipe, are contained in the tall derrick that is characteristic of rotary drilling rigs. While early derricks were constructed at the drilling site, modern rigs can be moved from one site to the next. The drill bit wears out quickly and requires frequent replacement, often once a day. This makes it necessary to pull the entire drill string from the well and stand all the joints of drill pipe vertically at one side of the derrick. Joints are usually nine metres long. While the bit is being changed, sections of two or three joints are separated and stacked. Drilling mud is left in the hole during this time to prevent excessive flow of fluids into the well.

CASING

Modern wells are not drilled to their total depth in a continuous process. Drilling may be stopped for logging and testing, and it also may be stopped to insert casing and cement it to the outer circumference of the bore-hole. Casing is steel pipe that is intended to prevent any transfer of fluids between the borehole and the surrounding formations. Since the drill bit must pass through any installed casing in order to continue drilling, the borehole below each string of casing is smaller than the borehole above. In very deep wells, as many as five intermediate strings of progressively smaller-diameter casing may be used during the drilling process.

DIRECTIONAL DRILLING

Frequently, the drilling platform and derrick cannot be located directly above the spot where the well should penetrate the formation (if, for example, petroleum reservoirs lie under lakes, towns, or harbours). In these cases, the surface equipment must be offset and the well bore drilled at an angle that will intersect the underground formation at the desired place. This is done by drilling the wells vertically to start and then angling them at depths that depend on the relative position of the target. Since the nearly inflexible drill pipe must be able to move and rotate through the entire depth, the angle of the borehole can be changed only a few degrees at any one time. In order to achieve a large deviation angle, therefore, a number of small deviations must be made. The borehole, in effect, ends up making a large arc to reach its objective.

The traditional tool for "kicking off" such a well is the whipstock. This consists of an inclined plane on the bottom of the drill pipe that is oriented in the direction the well is intended to take. The drill bit is thereby forced to move off in the proper direction. A more recent technique makes use of a "bent sub" at the bottom of the drill pipe that is pointed in the desired direction. A mud-powered turbine at the bottom of the sub drills the first few metres of the angled hole.

Directional drilling techniques have advanced to the point where well bores can end in horizontal sections extending into previously inaccessible areas of a reservoir. Also, multiple deposits can be accessed by a number of boreholes fanning out from a single surface structure.

Drilling Offshore

Many petroleum reservoirs are found in places where normal land-based drilling rigs cannot be used. In shallow inland waters or wetland areas, a drilling platform and other normal equipment may be mounted on a barge, which can be floated into position and then made to rest on the bottom. The actual drilling platform can be raised above the water on masts if necessary. Drilling and other operations on the well make use of an opening through the barge hull. This type of rig is generally restricted to water depths of 15 metres or less.

In shallow Arctic waters where drifting ice is a hazard for fixed platforms, artificial islands are constructed. Onshore in Arctic areas, permafrost makes drilling difficult because melting around and under the drill site makes the ground unstable. Here, too, artificial islands are built up with rock or gravel.

In deeper, more open waters over continental shelves, drilling is done from free-floating platforms or from platforms either made to rest on the bottom anchored in a semisubmersible arrangement. Floating rigs are most often used for exploratory drilling, while bottom-resting platforms are usually associated with the drilling of wells in an established field. One type of floating rig is the drill ship. This is an oceangoing vessel with a derrick mounted in the middle, over an opening for the drilling operation. The ship is usually held in position by six or more anchors, although some vessels are capable of precise maneuvering with directional thrust propellers. Even so, drill ships will roll and pitch from wave action, making the drilling difficult.

Fixed platforms, which rest on the seafloor, are very stable, although they cannot drill in water as deep as floating platforms can. The most popular type is called a jack-up rig. This is a floating (but not self-propelled) platform with legs that can be lifted high off the seafloor while the platform is towed to the drilling site. There the legs are cranked downward by a rack-and-pinion gearing system until they encounter the seafloor and actually raise the platform 10 to 20 metres above the surface. The bottoms of the legs are usually fastened to the seafloor with pilings. Other types of bottom-setting platforms may rest on rigid steel or concrete bases that are constructed onshore to the correct height. After being towed to the drilling site, flotation tanks built into the base are flooded, and the base sinks to the ocean floor. Storage tanks for produced oil may be built into the underwater base section.

A stable platform can be obtained in deep water with a semisubmersible design. In semisubmersible platforms, buoyancy is afforded by a hull that is entirely underwater, while the operational platform is held well above the surface on supports. Normal wave action affects the platforms very little. These vessels are also kept in place during drilling by either anchors or precise maneuvering. In some cases the platform is pulled down on the cables so that its buoyancy creates a tension in the cables that holds it firmly in place. Semisubmersible platforms can operate in water more than 1,500 metres (5,000 feet) deep.

For both fixed and floating rigs, the drill pipe must still transmit both rotary power and drilling mud to the bit. In addition, the mud must be returned to the platform for recirculation. In order to accomplish these functions through seawater, an outer casing, called a riser, must extend from the seafloor to the platform. Also, a guidance system (usually consisting of cables fastened to the seafloor) must be in place to allow equipment and tools from the surface to enter the well bore. In the case of floating platforms, there will always be some motion of the platform relative to the seafloor, so this equipment must be both flexible and extensible. A guidance system will be especially necessary if the well is to be put into production after the drilling platform is moved away.

WELL LOGGING AND DRILL-STEM TESTING

After the borehole has penetrated a potential productive zone, the formations must be tested to determine if expensive completion procedures should be used. The first evaluation is usually made using well-logging methods. The logging tool is lowered into the well by a steel cable and is pulled past the formations while response signals are relayed to the surface for observation and recording. Often these tools make use of the difference in electrical conductivities of rock, water, and petroleum to detect possible oil or gas accumulations. Other logging tools use differences in radioactivity, neutron absorption, and acoustic wave absorption. Well-log analysts can use the recorded signals to determine potential producing formations and their exact depth. Only a production test, however, can establish the potential productivity of a formation.

The production test normally employed is the drill-stem test, in which a testing tool is attached to the bottom of the drill pipe and is lowered to a point opposite the formation to be tested. The tool is equipped with expandable seals for isolating the formation from the rest of the borehole, and the drill pipe is emptied of mud so that formation fluid can enter. When enough time has passed, the openings into the tool are closed and the drill pipe is brought to the surface so that its contents may be measured. The amounts of oil and gas that flow into the drill pipe during the test and the recorded pressures are used to judge the production potential of the formation. (If there is gas present in the formation, the gas may flow from the top of the drill pipe during the test.) Similar tools are available that can seal off and test a formation in a cased well bore or that can bring a small sample of produced reservoir fluid to the surface at reservoir pressures.

WELL COMPLETION

If preliminary tests show that one or more of the formations penetrated by a borehole will be commercially productive, the well must be prepared for the continuous production of oil or gas. First, the casing is completed to

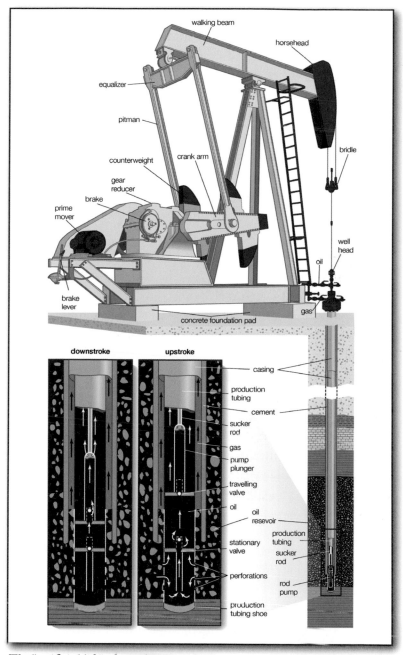

The "artificial lift" of petroleum, with a beam-pumping unit. Encyclopædia Britannica, Inc.

the bottom of the well. Cement is then forced into the annulus between the casing and the borehole wall to prevent fluid movement between formations. As mentioned earlier, this casing may be made up of progressively

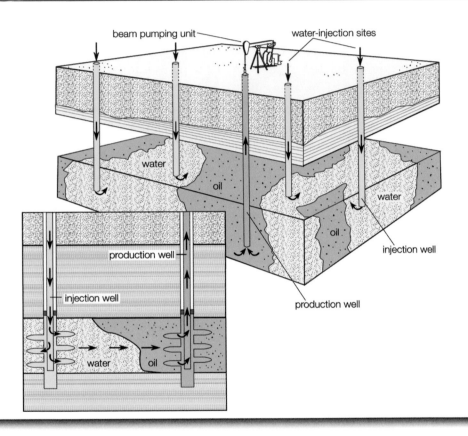

The recovery of petroleum through waterflooding. (Background) *Water is pumped into the oil reservoir from several sites around the field.* (Inset) *within the formation, the injected water forces oil toward the production well. Oil and water are pumped to the surface together.* From (inset) R. Baker, A Primer of Offshore Operations, 2nd ed., Petroleum Extension Service (PETEX), © 1985 The University of Texas at Austin, all rights reserved; R. Baker, Oil & Gas: The Production Story, Petroleum ExtensionService (PETEX), © 1983 The University of Texas at Austin, all rights reserved smaller-diameter tubing, so that the casing diameter at the bottom of the well may range from 10 to 30 cm (4 to 12 inches). After the casing is in place, a string of production tubing 5 to 10 cm (2 to 4 inches) in diameter is extended from the surface to the productive formation. Expandable packing devices are placed on the tubing to seal the annulus between the casing and the production tubing within the producing formation from the annulus within the remainder of the well. If several producing formations are penetrated by a single well, more than one production string may be hung. If a lifting device is needed to bring the oil to the surface, it is generally placed at the bottom of the production tubing.

Since the casing is sealed with cement against the productive formation, openings must be made in the casing wall and cement to allow formation fluid to enter the well. A perforator tool is lowered through the tubing on a wire line. When it is in the correct position, bullets are fired or explosive charges are set off to create an open path between the formation and the production string. If the formation is quite productive, these perforations, usually about 30 cm (12 inches) apart, will be sufficient to create a flow of fluid into the well. If not, an inert fluid may be injected into the formation at pressure high enough to cause fracturing of the rock around the well and thus open more flow passages for the petroleum. An acid that can dissolve portions of the rock is sometimes used in a similar manner.

When the subsurface equipment is in place, a network of valves, referred to as a Christmas tree, is installed at the top of the well. The valves regulate flow from the well and allow tools for subsurface work to be lowered through the tubing on a wire line. Christmas trees may be very simple, as in those found on low-pressure wells that must be pumped, or they may be very complex, as on high-pressure flowing wells with multiple producing strings.

RECOVERY OF OIL AND GAS

Petroleum reservoirs usually start with a formation pressure high enough to force crude oil into the well and sometimes to the surface through the tubing. However, since production is invariably accompanied by a decline in reservoir pressure, "primary recovery" through natural drive soon comes to an end. In addition, many oil reservoirs enter production with a formation pressure high enough to push the oil into the well but not up to the surface through the tubing. In these cases, some means of "artificial lift" must be installed. The most common installation uses a pump at the bottom of the production tubing that is operated by a motor and a "walking beam" (an arm that rises and falls like a seesaw) on the surface.

When a large part of the crude oil in a reservoir cannot be recovered by primary means, a method for supplying extra energy must be found. Most often, "secondary recovery" is accomplished by injecting gas or water into the reservoir to replace produced fluids and thus maintain or increase the reservoir pressure. An even more widely practiced secondary recovery method is waterflooding, in which water is injected through some of the wells in an oil field. It then moves through the formation, pushing oil toward the remaining production wells.

Although waterflooding greatly increases recovery from a particular reservoir, it still leaves up to one-third of the oil in place, prompting the industry to seek "enhanced methods" of recovering crude oil supplies. One method of enhanced recovery is based on the injection of natural gas; another involves putting a band of soaplike surfactant material ahead of the water. Heavy crude oils, which may be too viscous to produce well, can be heated by the injection of steam and then lifted to the surface. An alternate method for heating a reservoir, called in situ combustion, involves the combustion of a part of the reservoir oil to create hot combustion products that move through the reservoir to promote oil production. In situ combustion has not seen widespread use.

CHAPTER 3
PETROLEUM
REFINING

The extraction of petroleum from underground reservoirs, a gigantic effort in itself, is followed by the conversion of crude oil into useful products in a process known as refining.

THE HISTORY OF REFINING

In the early days of the petroleum industry in the 19th century, crude oil was merely subjected to a simple distillation treatment, in which lighter fractions of the oil were evaporated from heavier fractions and collected by

Petroleum refinery at Ras Tanura, Saudi Arabia. Herbert Lanks—Shostal

condensation. Modern petroleum industrial processes, however, bring about chemical changes, so that refining today is a complex process of separation, conversion, and purification.

DISTILLATION OF KEROSENE AND NAPHTHA

The refining of crude petroleum owes its origin to the successful drilling of the first oil well in Titusville, Pa., in 1859. Prior to that time, petroleum was available only in very small quantities from natural seepage of subsurface oil in various areas throughout the world. With the discovery of "rock oil" in northwestern Pennsylvania, crude oil became available in sufficient quantity to inspire the development of large-scale processing systems.

The earliest refineries employed simple distillation units, or "stills," to separate the various constituents of petroleum by heating the crude oil mixture in a vessel and condensing the resultant vapours into liquid fractions. Initially the primary product was kerosene, which proved to be a more abundant, cleaner-burning lamp oil of more consistent quality than whale oil or animal fat.

The lowest-boiling raw product from the still was "straight run" naphtha, a forerunner of unfinished gasoline. Its initial commercial application was primarily as a solvent. Higher-boiling materials were found to be effective as lubricants and fuel oils, but they were largely novelties at first.

The perfection of oil-drilling techniques quickly spread to Russia. By 1890 refineries there were producing large quantities of kerosene and fuel oils. The development of the internal-combustion engine in the later years of the 19th century created a small market for crude naphtha. But the development of the automobile at the turn of the century sharply increased the demand for quality gasoline, and this finally provided a home for the petroleum fractions that were too volatile to be included in kerosene. As demand for automotive fuel rose, methods for continuous distillation of crude oil were developed.

CONVERSION TO LIGHT FUELS

After 1910 the demand for automotive fuel began to outstrip the market requirements for kerosene, and refiners were pressed to develop new technologies to increase gasoline yields. The earliest process, called thermal cracking, consisted of heating heavier oils (for which there was a low market requirement) in pressurized reactors and thereby cracking, or splitting, their large molecules into the smaller ones that form the lighter, more valuable fractions such as gasoline, kerosene, and light industrial fuels. Gasoline manufactured by the cracking process performed better in automobile engines than gasoline derived from straight distillation of crude petroleum. The development of more powerful aircraft engines in the late 1930s gave rise to a need to increase the combustion characteristics of gasoline and spurred the development of lead-based fuel additives to improve engine performance.

During the 1930s and World War II, sophisticated refining processes involving the use of catalysts led to further improvements in the quality of transportation fuels and further increased their supply. These improved processes—including catalytic cracking of heavy oils, alkylation, polymerization, and isomerization—enabled the petroleum industry to meet the demands of high-performance combat aircraft and, after the war, to supply increasing quantities of transportation fuels.

The 1950s and '60s brought a large-scale demand for jet fuel and high-quality lubricating oils. The continuing increase in demand for petroleum products also heightened the need to process a wider variety of crude oils into high-quality products. Catalytic reforming of naphtha replaced the earlier thermal reforming process and became the leading process for upgrading fuel qualities to meet the needs of higher-compression engines. Hydrocracking, a catalytic cracking process conducted in the presence of hydrogen, was developed to be a versatile manufacturing process for increasing the yields of either gasoline or jet fuels.

THE RISE OF ENVIRONMENTAL CONCERNS

By 1970 the petroleum-refining industry had become well established throughout the world, with major concentrations of refineries in most developed countries. As the world became aware of the impact of industrial pollution on the environment, however, the petroleum-refining industry was a primary focus for change. Refiners added hydrotreating units to extract sulfur compounds from their products and began to generate large quantities of elemental sulfur. Effluent water and atmospheric emission of hydrocarbons and combustion products also became a focus of increased technical attention. In addition, many refined products came under scrutiny.

By the mid-1970s petroleum refiners in the United States were required to develop techniques for manufacturing high-quality gasoline without employing lead additives, and by 1990 they were required to take on substantial investments in the complete reformulation of transportation fuels in order to minimize environmental emissions. From an industry that produced a single product (kerosene) and disposed of unwanted by-product materials in any manner possible, petroleum refining had become one of the most stringently regulated of all manufacturing industries, expending a major portion of its resources on the protection of the environment.

PROPERTIES OF CRUDE OIL

Petroleum crude oils are complex mixtures of hydrocarbons, chemical compounds composed only of carbon (C) and hydrogen (H). In addition to the hydrocarbons, compounds of sulfur, nitrogen, and oxygen are present in small amounts in crude oils. Also there are usually traces of vanadium, nickel, chlorine, sodium, and arsenic. These elements may affect the safety of oil-transport systems, the quality of refined products, and the effectiveness of processing units within a refinery. Minute traces can usually be tolerated, but crudes with larger amounts of these materials must be extensively treated in order to restrict their harmful effects.

SATURATED HYDROCARBONS

The simplest of the hydrocarbon molecules is methane (CH_4), which has one carbon atom and four hydrogen atoms per molecule. The next simplest, ethane (C_2H_6), has two carbon atoms and six hydrogen atoms. A whole class of hydrocarbons can be defined by expanding upon the relationship between methane and ethane. Known as the paraffins, this is a family of chainlike molecules with the chemical formula CnH_{2n+2}. These molecules are also referred to as saturated, since each of the four valence electrons on a carbon atom that are available for bonding is taken up by a single hydrogen or carbon atom. Because these "single" bonds leave no valence electron available for sharing with another atom, paraffin molecules tend to be chemically stable.

H H H H
| | | |
H—C—C—C—C—H
| | | |
H H H H
butane
(paraffin)

cyclopentane
(naphthene)

H H
| |
H—C—C≡C
| | |
H H H
propylene
(olefin)

benzene
(aromatic)

© 1999 Encyclopædia Britannica, Inc.

Structures assumed by hydrogen (H) and carbon (C) molecules in four common hydrocarbon compounds. Encyclopædia Britannica, Inc.

Paraffins can be arranged either in straight chains (normal paraffins, such as butane) or branched chains (isoparaffins). Most of the paraffin compounds in naturally occurring crude oils are normal paraffins, while isoparaffins are frequently produced in refinery processes. The normal paraffins are uniquely poor as motor fuels, while isoparaffins have good engine-combustion characteristics. Longer-chain paraffins are major constituents of waxes.

Once a hydrocarbon molecule contains more than four carbon atoms, the carbon atoms may form not a branched or straight chain but a closed-ring structure known as a cyclo-compound. Saturated cyclo-compounds are called naphthenes. Naphthenic crudes tend to be poor raw materials for lubricant manufacture, but they are more easily converted into high-quality gasolines than are the paraffin compounds.

UNSATURATED HYDROCARBONS

Two other chemical families that are important in petroleum refining are composed of unsaturated molecules. In unsaturated molecules, not all the valence electrons on a carbon atom are bonded to separate carbon or hydrogen atoms; instead, two or three electrons may be taken up by one neighbouring carbon atom, thus forming a "double" or "triple" carbon-carbon bond. Like saturated compounds, unsaturated compounds can form either chain or ring molecules. Unsaturated chain molecules are known as olefins. Only small amounts of olefins are found in crude oils, but large volumes are produced in refining processes. Olefins are relatively reactive as chemicals and can be readily combined to form other longer-chain compounds.

The other family of unsaturated compounds is made up of ring molecules called aromatics. The simplest aromatic compound, benzene (C_6H_6), has double bonds linking every other carbon molecule. The double bonds in the benzene ring are very unstable and chemically reactive. Partly for this reason, benzene is a popular building block in the petrochemical industry.

Unsaturated hydrocarbons generally have good combustion characteristics, but their reactivity can lead to instability in storage and sometimes to environmental emission problems.

NONHYDROCARBON CONTENT

In addition to the practically infinite mixtures of hydrocarbon compounds that form crude oil, sulfur, nitrogen, and oxygen are usually present in small but often important quantities. Sulfur is the third most abundant atomic constituent of crude oils. It is present in the medium and heavy fractions of crude oils. In the low and medium molecular ranges, sulfur is associated only with carbon and hydrogen, while in the heavier fractions it is frequently incorporated in the large polycyclic molecules that also contain nitrogen and oxygen. The total sulfur in crude oil varies from below 0.05 percent (by weight), as in some Pennsylvania oils, to about 2 percent for average Middle Eastern crudes and up to 5 percent or more in heavy Mexican or Mississippi oils. Generally, the higher the specific gravity of the crude oil, the greater is its sulfur content. The excess sulfur is removed from crude oil during refining, because sulfur oxides released into the atmosphere during the combustion of oil would constitute a major pollutant.

The oxygen content of crude oil is usually less than 2 percent by weight and is present as part of the heavier hydrocarbon compounds in most cases. For this reason, the heavier oils contain the most oxygen. Nitrogen is present in almost all crude oils, usually in quantities of less than 0.1 percent by weight. Sodium chloride also occurs in most crudes and is usually removed like sulfur.

Many metallic elements are found in crude oils, including most of those that occur in seawater. This is probably due to the close association between seawater and the organic forms from which oil is generated. Among the most common metallic elements in oil are vanadium and nickel, which apparently occur in organic combinations as they do in living plants and animals.

Crude oil also may contain a small amount of decay-resistant organic remains, such as siliceous skeletal fragments, wood, spores, resins, coal, and various other remnants of former life.

TYPES OF CRUDE OIL

The above description of hydrocarbons refers to simpler members of each family, but crude oils are actually

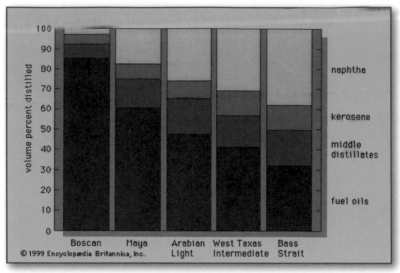

Product content of five major crude oils.

complex mixtures of very long-chain compounds, some of which have not yet been identified. Because such complex mixtures cannot be readily identified by chemical composition, refiners customarily characterize crude oils by the type of hydrocarbon compound that is most prevalent in them: paraffins, naphthenes, and aromatics. Some crude oils, such as those in the original Pennsylvanian oil fields, consist mainly of paraffins. Others, such as the heavy Mexican and Venezuelan crudes, are predominantly naphthenic and are rich in bitumen (a high-boiling semisolid material frequently made into asphalt for road surfaces).

Several products may be obtained by distillation of most crude oils, ranging from heavy Venezuelan Boscan to the light Bass Strait oil produced in Australia. However, given the pattern of modern demand (which tends to be highest for transportation fuels such as gasoline), the market price of a crude oil generally rises with increasing yields of light products. It is possible to process heavier crudes more intensely in order to improve their yield of light products, but the capital and operating costs required to support such high conversion processes are much greater than those required to process lighter crudes into the same yield of products.

CONVENTIONAL MEASUREMENT SYSTEMS

Petroleum refining is a continuous manufacturing process that is highly dependent on careful measurement of operating variables to influence product qualities and to control operating expenses. The conventional practice for the industry in the United States is to measure capacity by volume and to employ the English system for other operating measurements. Most refiners in other areas of the world define capacity by the weight of materials processed and record operating measurements in metric units. Since

MEASUREMENT SYSTEMS EMPLOYED IN PETROLEUM REFINING		
REFINERY OPERATION	UNITS OF MEASURE	
	INTERNATIONAL	U.S.
quantity processed	metric tons	barrels (42 gallons per barrel)
unit capacity	tons per year	barrels per day
flow rate	cubic metres per day	barrels per day
temperature	degrees Celsius	degrees Fahrenheit
pressure	kilograms per square centimetre	pounds per square inch
heat energy	joules or calories	British thermal units

many refiners throughout the world have U.S. shareholders, international results are often reported on both bases. In this chapter, all measurements will be presented in international terms with the U.S. equivalent indicated in parentheses.

BASIC REFINERY PROCESSES

Each refinery is uniquely designed to process specific crude oils into selected products. In order to meet the business objectives of the refinery, the process designer selects from an array of basic processing units. In general, these units perform one of three functions: (1) separating the many types of hydrocarbon present in crude oils into fractions of more closely related properties, (2) chemically converting the separated hydrocarbons into more desirable reaction products, and (3) purifying the products of unwanted elements and compounds. Following are descriptions of the most important processes for performing each of these functions.

SEPARATION: FRACTIONAL DISTILLATION

The primary process for separating the hydrocarbon components of crude oil is fractional distillation. Crude oil distillers separate crude oil into fractions for subsequent processing in such units as catalytic reformers, cracking units, alkylation units, or cokers. In turn, each of these more complex processing units also incorporates a fractional distillation tower to separate its own reaction products.

In a modern fractional distillation unit, crude oil is withdrawn from storage tanks at ambient temperature and pumped at a constant rate through a series of heat exchangers in order to reach a temperature of about 120 °C

(250 °F). A controlled amount of fresh water is introduced, and the mixture is pumped into a desalting drum, where it passes through an electrical field and a saltwater phase is separated. The desalted crude oil passes through additional heat exchangers and then through steel alloy tubes in a furnace. There it is heated to a temperature between 315 and 400 °C (600 and 750 °F), depending on the type of crude oil and the end products desired. A mixture of vapour and unvaporized oil passes from the furnace into the fractionating column, a vertical cylindrical tower as much as 45 metres (150 feet) high containing 20 to 40 fractionating trays spaced at regular intervals.

The oil vapours rise up through the column and are condensed to a liquid in a water- or air-cooled condenser at the top of the tower. A small amount of gas remains

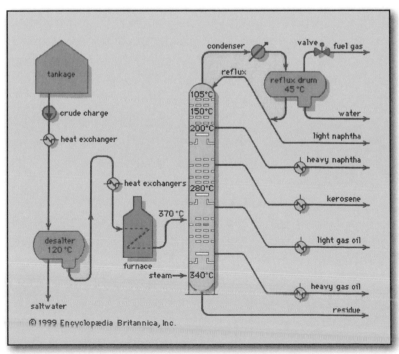

Schematic diagram of a crude-oil fractional distillation column.

uncondensed and is piped into the refinery fuel-gas system. Part of the condensed liquid, called reflux, is pumped back into the top of the column and descends from tray to tray, contacting rising vapours as they pass through the slots in the trays. The liquid progressively absorbs heavier constituents from the vapour and, in turn, gives up lighter constituents to the vapour phase. Condensation and reevaporation takes place on each tray. Eventually an equilibrium is reached in which there is a continual gradation of temperature and oil properties throughout the column, with the lightest constituents on the top tray and the heaviest on the bottom. The use of reflux and vapour-liquid contacting trays distinguishes fractional distillation from simple distillation columns.

Intermediate products, or "sidestreams," are withdrawn at several points from the column. In addition, modern crude distillation units employ intermediate reflux streams. Sidestreams are known as intermediate products because they have properties between those of the top or overhead product and those of products issuing from the base of the column. Typical boiling ranges for various streams are as follows: light straight-run naphtha (overhead), 20–95 °C (70–200 °F); heavy naphtha (top sidestream), 90–165 °C (195–330 °F); crude kerosene (second sidestream), 150–245 °C (300–475 °F); light gas oil (third sidestream), 215–315 °C (420–600 °F).

Unvaporized oil entering the column flows downward over a similar set of trays in the lower part of the column, called stripping trays, which act to remove any light constituents remaining in the liquid. Typically a single sidestream is withdrawn from the stripping section: heavy gas oil, with a boiling range of 285–370 °C (545–700 °F). The residue that passes from the bottom of the column is suitable for blending into industrial fuels or for manufacture into lubricating oils.

CONVERSION: CATALYTIC CRACKING

All petroleum refineries throughout the world employ at least crude oil distillation units to separate naturally occurring fractions for further use, but those which employ distillation alone are limited in their yield of valuable transportation fuels. By adding more complex conversion processes that chemically change the molecular structure of naturally occurring components of crude oil, it is possible to increase the yield of valuable hydrocarbon compounds.

The use of thermal cracking units to convert gas oils into naphtha dates from before 1920. These units produced small quantities of unstable naphthas and large amounts of by-product coke. While they succeeded in providing a small increase in gasoline yields, it was the commercialization of the fluid catalytic cracking process in 1942 that really established the foundation of modern petroleum refining. The process not only provided a highly efficient means of converting high-boiling gas oils into naphtha to meet the rising demand for high-octane gasoline, but it also represented a breakthrough in catalyst technology.

The thermal cracking process functioned largely in accordance with the free-radical theory of molecular transformation. Under conditions of extreme heat, the electron bond between carbon atoms in a hydrocarbon molecule can be broken, thus generating a hydrocarbon group with an unpaired electron. This negatively charged molecule, called a free radical, enters into reactions with other hydrocarbons, continually producing other free radicals via the transfer of negatively charged hydride ions (H^-). Thus a chain reaction is established that leads to a reduction in molecular size, or "cracking," of components of the original feedstock.

Use of a catalyst in the cracking reaction increases the yield of high-quality products under much less severe operating conditions than in thermal cracking. Several complex reactions are involved, but the principal mechanism by which long-chain hydrocarbons are cracked into lighter products can be explained by the carbonium ion theory. According to this theory, a catalyst promotes the removal of a negatively charged hydride ion from a paraffin compound or the addition of a positively charged proton (H^+) to an olefin compound. This results in the formation of a carbonium ion, a positively charged molecule that has only a very short life as an intermediate compound which transfers the positive charge through the hydrocarbon. Carbonium transfer continues as hydrocarbon compounds come into contact with active sites on the surface of the catalyst that promote the continued

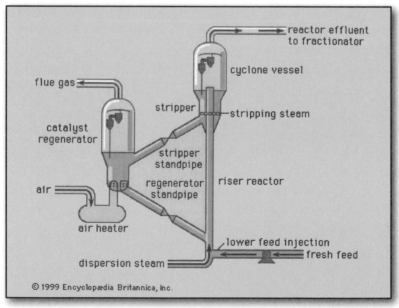

Schematic diagram of a fluid catalytic cracking unit. Encyclopædia Britannica, Inc.

addition of protons or removal of hydride ions. The result is a weakening of carbon-carbon bonds in many of the hydrocarbon molecules and a consequent cracking into smaller compounds.

Typical modern catalytic cracking reactors operate at 480–550 °C (900–1,020 °F) and at relatively low pressures of 0.7 to 1.4 kg per square cm (10 to 20 pounds per square inch). At first natural silica-alumina clays were used as catalysts, but by the mid-1970s zeolitic and molecular sieve-based catalysts became common. Zeolitic catalysts give more selective yields of products while reducing the formation of gas and coke.

A modern fluid catalytic cracker employs a finely divided solid catalyst that has properties analogous to a liquid when it is agitated by air or oil vapours. In a typical arrangement a reactor and regenerator are located side by side. The oil feed is vaporized when it meets the hot catalyst at the feed-injection point, and the vapours flow upward through the riser reactor at high velocity, providing a fluidizing effect for the catalyst particles. The catalytic reaction occurs exclusively in the riser reactor. The catalyst then passes into the cyclone vessel, where it is separated from reactor hydrocarbon products.

The cracked reactor effluent is fractionated in a distillation column. The yield of light products (with boiling points less than 220 °C, or 430 °F) is usually reported as the conversion level for the unit. Conversion levels are usually higher in the United States than they are in Europe and Asia. In the United States about one-third of the product yield consists of fuel gas and other gaseous hydrocarbons. Half of this is usually propylene and butylene, which are important feedstocks for further processing. The largest volume is usually cracked naphtha, an important gasoline blend stock with an octane number of 90 to 94. The lower conversion units of Europe and Asia produce comparatively more distillate oil and less naphtha and light hydrocarbons.

PURIFICATION

Before petroleum products can be marketed, certain impurities must be removed or made less obnoxious. The most common impurities are sulfur compounds such as hydrogen sulfide (H_2S) or the mercaptans ("R"SH)—the latter being a series of complex organic compounds having as many as six carbon atoms in the hydrocarbon radical ("R"). Apart from their foul odour, sulfur compounds are technically undesirable. In motor and aviation fuels they reduce the effectiveness of antiknock additives and interfere with the operation of exhaust-treatment systems. In diesel fuel they cause engine corrosion and complicate exhaust-treatment systems. Also, many major residual and industrial fuel consumers are located in developed areas and are subject to restrictions on sulfurous emissions.

Other undesirable components include nitrogen compounds, which poison catalyst systems, and oxygenated compounds, which can lead to colour formation and product instability.

Several treatment processes are employed for purifying products, including: oxidizing mercaptans to more innocuous disulfides, which can remain in the fuel; treating with clay to remove gum and gum-forming materials; combining the product with hydrogen over a catalyst to convert sulfur to hydrogen sulfide, which can be removed from the stream; and passing the product through a "molecular sieve" such as zeolite, which adsorbs impurities such as water, carbon dioxide, hydrogen sulfide, and mercaptans.

CHAPTER 4

NATURAL GAS

Natural gas is a colourless, highly flammable gaseous hydrocarbon consisting primarily of methane and ethane. It is a type of petroleum that commonly occurs in association with crude oil. Natural gas is often found dissolved in oil at the high pressures existing in a reservoir, and it also can be present as a gas cap above the oil. In fact, in many instances it is the pressure of natural gas exerted upon the subterranean oil reservoir that provides the force to drive oil up to the surface. Such natural gas is known as associated gas. There are also reservoirs that contain gas and no oil. This gas is termed nonassociated gas.

Associated gas usually contains some light liquids and hence is sometimes called "wet gas." "Dry gas" comes from the reservoirs that are not connected with any known source of liquid petroleum.

ORIGINS OF NATURAL GAS

Natural gas is more ubiquitous than oil. It is derived from both land plants and aquatic organic matter and is generated above, throughout, and below the oil window. Thus, all source rocks have the potential for gas generation. Many of the source rocks for significant gas deposits appear to be associated with the worldwide occurrence of coal dated to Carboniferous and Early Permian times (roughly 360 million to 271 million years ago).

ORGANIC FORMATION

During the immature, or biological, stage of petroleum formation, biogenic methane (often called marsh gas) is produced as a result of the decomposition of organic material by the action of anaerobic microbes. These microorganisms cannot tolerate even traces of oxygen and are also inhibited by high concentrations of dissolved sulfate. Consequently, biogenic gas generation is confined to certain environments that include poorly drained swamps and bays, some lake bottoms, and marine environments beneath the zone of active sulfate reduction. Gas of predominantly biogenic origin is thought to constitute more than 20 percent of the world's gas reserves.

The mature stage of petroleum generation, which occurs at depths of about 750 to 5,000 metres (2,500 to 16,000 feet), includes the full range of hydrocarbons that are produced within the oil window. Often significant amounts of thermal methane gas are generated along with the oil. Below 2,900 metres (9,500 feet), primarily wet gas (gas containing liquid hydrocarbons) is formed.

In the postmature stage, below about 5,000 metres, oil is no longer stable, and the main hydrocarbon product is thermal methane gas. Those hydrocarbons with a larger chemical structure than that of methane are destroyed much more rapidly than they are formed. Thus, in the sedimentary basins of the world, comparatively little oil is found below 5,000 metres. The deep basins with thick sequences of sedimentary rocks, however, have the potential for deep gas production.

INORGANIC FORMATION

Some methane may have been produced by inorganic processes. The original source of the Earth's carbon was the cosmic debris from which the planet formed. If meteorites are representative of this debris, the carbon could have been supplied in comparatively high concentrations as hydrocarbons, such as are found in the carbonaceous chondrite type of meteorites. Continuous outgassing of these hydrocarbons may be taking place from within the Earth, and some may have accumulated as abiogenic gas deposits without having passed through an organic phase. In the event of widespread outgassing, however, it is likely that abiogenic gas would be too diffuse to be of commercial interest. Significant accumulations of inorganic methane have yet to be found.

The helium and some of the argon found in natural gas are products of natural radioactive disintegration. Helium derives from radioisotopes of thorium and the uranium family, and argon derives from potassium. It is probably coincidental that helium and argon sometimes occur with natural gas. In all likelihood, the unrelated gases simply became caught in the same trap.

THE GEOLOGIC ENVIRONMENT

Like oil, natural gas migrates and accumulates in traps. Oil accumulations contain more recoverable energy than gas accumulations of similar size, even though the recovery of gas is a more efficient process than the recovery of oil. This is due to the differences in the physical and chemical properties of gas and oil. Gas displays initial low concentration and high dispersibility, making adequate cap rocks very important.

Natural gas can be the primary target of either deep or shallow drilling because large gas accumulations form above the oil window as a result of biogenic processes and thermal gas occurs throughout and below the oil window. In most sedimentary basins the vertical potential (and

A worker power-washes equipment on the drilling site of a well (tower to the right) in the Marcellus Shale, an extensive gas-containing formation in the northeastern United States. Bloomberg via Getty Images

sediment volume) available for gas generation exceeds that of oil. About a quarter of the known major gas fields are related to a shallow biogenic origin, but most major gas fields are located at intermediate or deeper levels where higher temperatures and older reservoirs (often carbonates sealed by evaporites) exist.

GAS RESERVOIRS

Gas reservoirs differ greatly, with different physical variations affecting reservoir performance and recovery. In a natural gas (single-phase) reservoir it should be possible to recover nearly all of the in-place gas by dropping the pressure sufficiently. If the pressure is effectively maintained

UNCONVENTIONAL GAS RESERVOIRS

Substantial amounts of gas have accumulated in geologic environments that differ from conventional petroleum traps. This gas is termed unconventional gas and occurs in "tight" (i.e., relatively impermeable) sandstones, in joints and fractures or absorbed into the matrix of shales (often of the Devonian Period, about 416 million to 359 million years ago), dissolved or entrained in hot geopressured formation waters, and in coal seams. Unconventional gas sources are much more expensive to exploit and have to be produced at much slower rates than conventional gas fields. Moreover, recoveries are low. In all likelihood, unconventional gas will continue to complement conventional gas production but will not supplant it.

Tight gas occurs in either blanket or lenticular sandstones that have an effective permeability of less than 1 millidarcy (or 0.001 darcy, which is the standard unit of permeability of a substance to fluid flow). These relatively impermeable sandstones are reservoirs for considerable amounts of gas that are mostly uneconomical to produce because of low natural flow rates. The outlook for increased production of gas from tight sandstones has been enhanced by the use of massive hydraulic fracturing techniques that create large collection areas in low-permeability formations through which gas can flow to a producing well. A fractured well in a tight gas formation usually produces at a lower rate than a conventional gas well but for a longer time.

Devonian shale gas was generated from organic mud deposited during the Devonian Period. Subsequent sedimentation and the resultant heat and pressure transformed the mud into shale and also produced natural gas from the organic matter contained therein. Some of the gas migrated to adjacent sandstones and was trapped in them, forming conventional gas accumulations. The rest of the gas remained locked in the nonporous shale. The production history of Devonian shale gas indicates that the recovered gas occurs in well-connected fracture porosity. Production is generally at low flow rates but is long-lasting.

> The factor of greatest importance in commercial production is the presence of natural fractures, but wells can be stimulated by explosives or by hydraulic fracturing, which sometimes enhances gas production.

by the encroachment of water in the sedimentary rock formation, however, some of the gas will be lost to production by being trapped by capillarity behind the advancing water front. Therefore, in practice, only about 80 percent of the in-place gas can be recovered. On the other hand, if the pressure declines, there is an economic limit at which the cost of compression exceeds the value of the recovered gas. Depending on formation permeability, actual gas recovery can be as high as 75 to 80 percent of the original in-place gas in the reservoir. Associated gas is produced along with the oil and separated at the surface.

HISTORY OF THE USE OF NATURAL GAS

Although the widespread use of natural gas is a fairly recent phenomenon, its use predates the industrial era.

The first discoveries of natural gas seeps were made in what is today Iran between 6000 and 2000 BCE. Many early writers described the natural petroleum seeps in the Middle East, especially in the Baku region of what is now Azerbaijan. The gas seeps, probably first ignited by lightning, provided the fuel for the "eternal fires" of the fire-worshiping religion of the ancient Persians.

The use of natural gas was mentioned in China about 900 BCE. It was in China in 211 BCE that the first known well was drilled for natural gas to reported depths of 150

A

MEETING

Of the Inhabitants of the

BOROUGH OF BERKELEY,

WILL BE HELD AT THE

BERKELEY ARMS HOTEL,

On TUESDAY Evening Next,

At Six o'Clock,

To consider the propriety and possibility of Lighting the Town with

GAS.

WILLIAM GAISFORD,

MAYOR.

Berkeley 21st January, 1854.

POVEY, PRINTER, BERKELEY.

A 19th-century notice concerning a town meeting in Berekeley, England to discuss using gaslit streetlamps. Some townships were wary about switching from oil or coal gas to natural gas. SSPL via Getty Images

metres (500 feet). The Chinese drilled their wells with bamboo poles and primitive percussion bits for the express purpose of searching for gas in limestones dating to the Late Triassic (about 229 million to 200 million years ago) in an anticline west of modern Chungking. The gas was burned to dry the rock salt found interbedded in the limestone. Eventually wells were drilled to depths approaching 1,000 metres (3,300 feet), and more than 1,100 wells had been drilled into the anticline by 1900.

Natural gas was unknown in Europe until its discovery in England in 1659, and even then it did not come into wide use. Instead, gas obtained from carbonized coal (known as town gas) became the primary fuel for illuminating streets and houses throughout much of Europe beginning in 1790. In North America the first commercial application of a petroleum product was the utilization of natural gas from a shallow well in Fredonia, N.Y., in 1821. The gas was distributed through a small-bore lead pipe to consumers for lighting and cooking.

IMPROVEMENTS IN GAS PIPELINES

Throughout the 19th century the use of natural gas remained localized because there was no way to transport large quantities of gas over long distances. Natural gas remained on the sidelines of industrial development, which was based primarily on coal and oil. An important breakthrough in gas-transportation technology occurred in 1890 with the invention of leakproof pipeline coupling. Nonetheless, materials and construction techniques remained so cumbersome that gas could not be used more than 160 km (100 miles) from a source of supply. Thus, associated gas was mostly flared (i.e., burned at the wellhead), and nonassociated gas was left in the ground, while town gas was manufactured for use in the cities.

Long-distance gas transmission became practical during the late 1920s because of further advances in pipeline technology. From 1927 to 1931, more than 10 major transmission systems were constructed in the United States.

Each of these systems was equipped with pipes having diameters of approximately 50 cm (20 inches) and extended more than 320 km (200 miles). Following World War II, a large number of even longer pipelines of increasing diameter were constructed. The fabrication of pipes having a diameter of up to 150 cm (60 inches) became possible. Since the early 1970s the longest gas pipelines have had their origin in Russia. For example, in the 1960s and '70s the 5,470-km (3,400-mile)-long Northern Lights pipeline was built across the Ural Mountains and some 700 rivers and streams, linking eastern Europe with the West Siberian gas fields on the Arctic Circle.

As a result, gas from Russia's Urengoy field, the world's largest, is now transported to eastern Europe and then on to western Europe for consumption. Another gas pipeline, shorter but also of great engineering difficulty, was the 50-cm (20-inch) Trans-Mediterranean Pipeline, which during the 1970s and '80s was extended from Algeria to Sicily. The sea is more than 600 metres deep along some parts of the route.

NATURAL GAS AS A PREMIUM FUEL

As recently as 1960, associated gas was a nuisance by-product of oil production in many areas of the world. The gas was separated from the crude oil stream and eliminated as cheaply as possible, often by flaring. Only after the crude oil shortages of the late 1960s and early 1970s did natural gas become an important world energy source.

In the United States the home-heating market for natural gas was limited until the 1930s, when town gas began to be replaced by abundant and cheaper supplies of natural gas, which contained twice the heating value of its synthetic predecessor. Also, when natural gas burns

LPG

Liquefied petroleum gas is a liquid mixture of the volatile hydro-carbons propene, propane, butene, and butane. LPG was used as early as 1860 for a portable fuel source, and its production and consumption for both domestic and industrial use have expanded ever since. A typical commercial mixture may also contain ethane and ethylene as well as a volatile mercaptan, an odorant added as a safety precaution.

LPG is recovered from "wet" natural gas (gas with condensable heavy petroleum compounds) by absorption. The recovered product has a low boiling point and must be distilled to remove the lighter fractions and then be treated to remove hydrogen sulfide, carbon dioxide, and water. The finished product is transported by pipeline and by specially built seagoing tankers. Transportation by truck, rail, and barge has also developed, particularly in the United States.

LPG reaches the domestic consumer in cylinders under relatively low pressures. The largest part of the LPG produced is used in central heating systems and the next largest as raw material for chemical plants; LPG is also used as an engine fuel.

completely, carbon dioxide and water are normally formed. The combustion of gas is relatively free of soot, carbon monoxide, and the nitrogen oxides associated with the burning of other fossil fuels. In addition, sulfur dioxide emissions, another major air pollutant, are almost nonexistent. As a consequence, natural gas is often a preferred fuel for environmental reasons.

PROPERTIES OF NATURAL GAS

Natural gas components are either gaseous or liquid hydrocarbons, often found in association with substantial quantities of nonhydrocarbon substances such as hydrogen sulfide. These compounds give natural gas various properties that make it a valuable fuel and a versatile raw material.

HYDROCARBON CONTENT

Natural gas is a hydrocarbon mixture consisting primarily of methane and ethane, both of which are gaseous under atmospheric conditions. The mixture also may contain other hydrocarbons, such as propane, butane, pentane, and hexane. In natural gas reservoirs even the heavier hydrocarbons occur for the most part in gaseous form because of the higher pressures. They liquefy at the surface (at atmospheric pressure) and are referred to as natural gas liquids, gas condensate, natural gasoline, or liquefied petroleum gas. They may separate in some reservoirs through retrograde condensation or may be separated at the surface either in field separators or in gas processing plants by means of condensation, absorption, adsorption, or other modification. The average production of natural gas liquids in the United States is nearly 38 barrels per 1 million cubic feet of produced gas.

NONHYDROCARBON CONTENT

Other gases that commonly occur in association with the hydrocarbon gases are nitrogen, carbon dioxide, hydrogen, hydrogen sulfide, and such noble gases as helium and argon. Because natural gas and formation water occur together in the reservoir, gas recovered from a well contains water vapour, which is partially condensed during transmission to the processing plant.

PHYSICAL PROPERTIES

The physical properties of natural gas include colour, odour, and flammability. The principal ingredient of gas is methane, which is colourless, odourless, and highly flammable. However, some of the associated gases in natural gas, especially hydrogen sulfide, have a distinct and penetrating odour, and a few parts per million is sufficient to impart a decided odour to natural gas.

MEASUREMENT SYSTEMS

The amounts of gas accumulated in a reservoir, as well as produced from wells, are calculated in cubic metres at a pressure of 750 mm of mercury and a temperature of 15 °C

A welder repairs a Siberian natural gas pipeline owned by Russian energy company OAO Gazprom. Siberia is home to some of the largest deposits of natural gas. Bloomberg via Getty Images

(or in cubic feet at an absolute pressure of 14.73 pounds per square inch and a temperature of 60 °F). Since gas is compressed at high reservoir pressures, it expands upon reaching the surface and thus occupies more space. As its quantity is calculated in reference to standard conditions of temperature and pressure, however, the expansion does not constitute an increase in the amount of gas produced.

WORLD DISTRIBUTION OF NATURAL GAS

The largest natural gas fields are the supergiants, which contain more than 850 billion cubic metres (30 trillion cubic feet) of gas, and the world-class giants, which have reserves of roughly 85 billion to 850 billion cubic metres (3 trillion to 30 trillion cubic feet). Supergiants and world-class giants represent less than 1 percent of the world's total known gas fields, but they originally contained, along with associated gas in giant oil fields, approximately 80 percent of the world's reserves and produced gas.

RUSSIA

Russia has the largest natural gas reserves in the world (some 47 trillion cubic metres [1,680 trillion cubic feet]) and is the world's largest producer (between 56 and 70 billion cubic metres [20 and 25 trillion cubic feet] per year) of natural gas. Some of the world's largest gas fields occur in a region of West Siberia east of the Gulf of Ob on the Arctic Circle.

Russia's largest gas field is Urengoy, which was discovered in 1966 and was estimated to have initial reserves as great as 8.1 trillion cubic metres (286 trillion cubic feet). Roughly three-quarters of this gas is found in the shallowest reservoir, 1,100 to 1,250 metres (3,600 and 4,100 feet) deep, which is Upper Cretaceous in age (from about 65.5 million to 100 million years old). In all, Urengoy has 15 separate reservoirs, some in Lower Cretaceous rocks (those that are approximately 100 million to 146 million years old). The deepest is a gas condensate zone in Upper Jurassic strata (from about 146 million to 161 million years old). Urengoy began production in 1978, and, though its output has declined over its peak years, it still exceeds the production from any other gas field in the world.

Yamburg, Russia's second largest gas field, was discovered north of the Arctic Circle and north of Urengoy. Its original reserves were estimated at 4.7 trillion cubic metres (166 trillion cubic feet) of gas, mostly from Upper Cretaceous reservoir rocks at depths of 1,000 to 1,210 metres (3,300 to 4,000 feet). Development of Yamburg began in the early 1980s.

Orenburg, discovered in the Volga-Urals region in 1967, is the largest Russian gas field outside of West Siberia. It had initial reserves of close to 1.8 trillion cubic metres (64 trillion cubic feet) of gas and began production in 1974.

EUROPE

The largest natural gas field in Europe is Groningen, with original recoverable reserves of about 2.27 trillion cubic metres (80 trillion cubic feet). It was discovered in 1959 on the Dutch coast. The discovery well was drilled through evaporites of Permian age (about 251 million to 299 million years old) into a thick basal Permian sandstone that was gas-productive. Subsequent drilling outlined a broad anticline about 24 km (15 miles) wide by 40 km (24 miles) long, which has a continuous basal Permian sandstone reservoir capped by evaporites. The reservoir contains natural gas at depths between 2,440 and 3,050 metres (8,000 and 10,000 feet). It overlies the truncated and strongly faulted coal-bearing Pennsylvanian sequence (the Pennsylvanian Period extended from about 318 million to 299 million years ago), which is considered to be the main source of the gas.

NORTH AMERICA

The United States has proven natural gas reserves of 6.6 trillion cubic metres (238 trillion cubic feet). Its largest gas field (Hugoton, discovered in 1927 in Kansas and found to extend through the Oklahoma and Texas panhandles) has an estimated ultimate recovery of 1.5 trillion cubic metres (54 trillion cubic feet), of which some 65 percent has been produced. More than 10,000 wells have been drilled in this extensive field, which produces from a series of Permian limestones and dolomites. The gas accumulations are stratigraphically controlled by variations in lithology. The productive area extends along a 400-km (240-mile) trend.

Canada has an estimated 1.6 trillion cubic metres (58 trillion cubic feet) of proven natural gas reserves. Its undiscovered resource potential is almost equal to that of the United States. The largest gas field is Elmworth. Discovered in Alberta in 1976, Elmworth contained some 560 billion cubic metres of gas in a Cretaceous sandstone reservoir.

Mexico's proven natural gas reserves amount to some 370 billion cubic metres (13.2 trillion cubic feet). Its gas production is spread throughout the country, much of it coming from the Canterell oil field in the Gulf of Mexico. Although Mexico's estimated proven reserves of gas are less than half those of Canada, natural gas is underutilized in Mexico, with billions of cubic metres of associated gas being flared every year at petroleum production facilities.

NORTH AFRICA

In North Africa the central basin of Algeria is the location of the Hassi R'Mel gas and condensate field. Discovered in 1956 in a large anticline, the field is estimated to have originally contained about 2.52 trillion cubic metres (89 trillion cubic feet) of recoverable gas in reservoirs of permeable Triassic sandstone (from about 200 million to 251 million years old) capped by salt beds. Hassi R'Mel produces some 42 billion cubic metres (1.5 trillion cubic feet) of gas per year, about half of Algeria's total dry-gas production.

MIDDLE EAST

There is an enormous gas potential in the Middle East associated with the major structures in the Arabian-Iranian basin. The Permian Khuff formation underlies most of the region and is an important gas-bearing horizon. Indeed, it forms the reservoir of the world's largest oil field, the supergiant North Field of offshore Qatar and South Pars of offshore Iran, which is estimated to contain more than 28 trillion cubic metres (1,000 trillion cubic feet) of reserves. On the basis of such reserves, Iran and Qatar are the second and third largest natural gas producers in the world, behind Russia.

ASIA

The largest gas field in Asia is Arun, which was discovered in 1971 in the North Sumatra basin of Indonesia. The gas reservoir is a reef limestone that dates to the middle of the

Miocene Epoch (some 16 million to 11 million years ago). Original reserves have been estimated at about 383 billion cubic metres (13.5 trillion cubic feet). The gas is liquefied for export.

USES OF NATURAL GAS

The largest single application for natural gas is as a domestic or industrial fuel. However, several specialized applications have developed over the years. The clean-burning characteristics of natural gas have made it a frequent choice as a nonpolluting transportation fuel. Buses and commercial automotive fleets now operate on compressed natural gas in many areas of the United States. Carbon black, a pigment of colloidal dimensions, is made by burning natural gas with a limited supply of air and depositing the soot on a cool surface. It is an important ingredient in dyes and inks and is used in rubber compounding operations.

More than half of the world's ammonia supply now is manufactured via a catalytic process from methane. It is used directly as a plant food or converted into a variety of chemicals such as hydrogen cyanide, nitric acid, urea, and a range of fertilizers.

A wide array of other chemical products can be made from natural gas by a controlled oxidation process—for example, methanol, propanol, and formaldehyde, which serve as basic materials for a wide range of other chemical products. Methanol can be used as a gasoline additive or gasoline substitute. In addition, methyl tertiary butyl ether (MTBE), an oxygenated fuel additive added to gasoline in response to environmental regulations in the United States, is produced via chemical reaction of methanol and isobutylene over an acidic ion-exchange resin.

Much of the world's supply of MTBE is dependent on the availability of isobutylene from refinery catalytic cracking units or olefin-manufacturing units in petrochemical plants. However, it is possible to base the process entirely on natural gas by processing NGLs through isomerization units and butane dehydrogenation facilities in order to produce isobutylene and then separately convert methane from the dry gas to methanol. Then the process would proceed as described above, reacting the methanol and isobutylene over an acidic ion-exchange resin to produce the MTBE product.

CHAPTER 5
COAL

Coal is a solid, usually brown or black, carbon-rich material that most often occurs in stratified sedimentary deposits. One of the most important of the primary fossil fuels, it is an abundant natural resource that can be used as a source of energy, as a chemical feedstock from which numerous synthetic compounds (e.g., dyes, oils, waxes, pharmaceuticals, and pesticides) can be derived, and in the production of coke for metallurgical processes. Coal is a major source of energy in the production of electrical power using steam generation. In addition, gasification and liquefaction produce gaseous and liquid fuels that can be easily transported (e.g., by pipeline) and conveniently stored in tanks.

Noted coal geologist James Morton Schopf defined coal as containing more than 50 percent by weight (or 70 percent by volume) carbonaceous matter produced by the compaction and induration of altered plant remains — namely, peat deposits. Different varieties of coal arise because of differences in the kinds of plant material (coal type), degree of coalification (coal rank), and range of impurities (coal grade). Although most coals occur in stratified sedimentary deposits, the deposits may later be subjected to elevated temperatures and pressures caused by igneous intrusions or deformation during orogenesis (i.e., processes of mountain building), resulting in the development of anthracite and even graphite. Although the concentration of carbon in the Earth's crust does not exceed 0.1 percent by weight, it is indispensable to life and constitutes humankind's main source of energy.

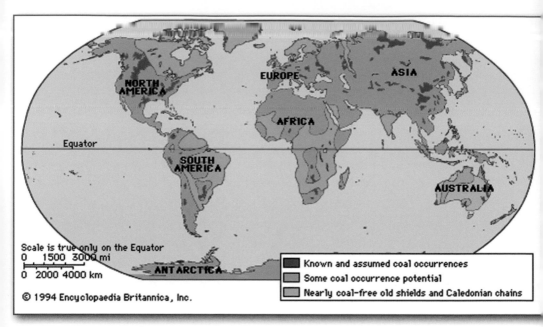

Location of the most-important coal occurrences on Earth.

THE ORIGINS OF COAL

Coal is especially worthy of the name fossil fuel, as it frequently bears visible traces of the geologic time period in which it has its origin. The journey from those ancient origins to the modern coke or reprocessing plant is hundreds of millions of years long.

PLANT MATTER

It is generally accepted that most coals formed from plants that grew in and adjacent to swamps in warm, humid regions. Material derived from these plants accumulated in low-lying areas that remained wet most of the time and was converted to peat through the activity of microorganisms. (It should be noted that peat can occur in temperate regions [e.g., Ireland and the state of Michigan in the United States] and even in subarctic regions [e.g., the Scandinavian countries].) Under certain conditions this organic material continued to accumulate and was later converted into coal.

Much of the plant matter that accumulates on the surface of the Earth is never converted to peat or to coal, because it is removed by fire or organic decomposition.

Lignite coal with fern fossilization. Runk/Schoenberger— Grant Heilman Photography

Hence, the vast coal deposits found in ancient rocks must represent periods during which several favourable biological and physical processes occurred at the same time.

Evidence that coal was derived from plants comes from three principal sources. First, lignites, the lowest coal rank, often contain recognizable plant remains. Second, sedimentary rock layers above, below, and adjacent to coal seams contain plant fossils in the form of impressions and carbonized films (e.g., leaves and stems) and casts of larger parts such as roots, branches, and trunks. Third, even coals of advanced rank may reveal the presence of precursor plant material. When examined microscopically in thin sections or polished blocks, cell walls, cuticles (the outer wall of leaves), spores, and other structures can still be recognized. Algal and fungal remains also may be present. (Algae are major components in boghead coal, a type of sapropelic coal.)

THE FOSSIL RECORD

Anthracite (the highest coal rank) material, which appears to have been derived from algae, is known from the Proterozoic Eon of Precambrian time (approximately 540 million to 2.5 billion years ago). Siliceous rocks of the same age contain fossil algae and fungi. These early plants were primarily protists (solitary or aggregate unicellular organisms that include yellow-green algae, golden-brown algae, and diatoms) that lived in aqueous environments. It was not until the Late Silurian Period (approximately 420 million years ago) that plants are known to have developed the ability to survive on land. Fossil organisms that are reflective of this dramatic evolutionary event have been discovered in Wales and Australia.

Evidence for early coastal forests is preserved in strata of the Late Devonian Period (approximately 360 to 385 million years old). By the latter half of the Paleozoic Era, plants had undergone extensive evolution and occupied many previously vacant environments. This phenomenon is sometimes called adaptive radiation.

There were two major eras of coal formation in geologic history. The older includes the Carboniferous Period (sometimes divided into the Mississippian and Pennsylvanian periods, from approximately 300 to 360 million years ago) and the Permian Period (from approximately 250 to 300 million years ago). Much of the bituminous coal of eastern North America and Europe is Carboniferous in age. Most coals in Siberia, eastern Asia, and Australia are of Permian origin. The younger era began about 135 million years ago during the Cretaceous Period and reached its peak approximately 2.6 to 65.5 million years ago, during the Paleogene and Neogene periods of the Cenozoic Era. Most of the coals that formed during this second era are lignites and subbituminous (or brown) coals. These are widespread in

Pennsylvanian coal forest diorama. The lone tree with horizontal grooves in the right foreground is a jointed sphenopsid (Calamites); *the large trees with scar patterns are lycopsids.* Courtesy of the Department Library Services, American Museum of Natural History, neg. #333983

such areas as western North America (including Alaska), southern France and central Europe, Japan, and Indonesia.

Late Paleozoic flora included sphenopsids, lycopsids, pteropsids, and the Cordaitales. The sphenopsid *Calamites* grew as trees in swamps. *Calamites* had long, jointed stems with sparse foliage. The lycopsids included species of *Lepidodendron* and *Sigillaria* (up to 30 metres [about 100 feet] tall) that grew in somewhat drier areas. Pteropsids included both true ferns (Filicineae) and extinct seed ferns (Pteridospermaphyta), which grew in relatively dry environments. The Cordaitales, which had tall stems and long, narrow, palmlike leaves, also favoured drier areas. During the Cretaceous and Cenozoic the angiosperms (flowering plants) evolved, producing a diversified flora from which the younger coals developed.

PEAT

Although peat is used as a source of energy, it is not usually considered a coal. It is the precursor material from which coals are derived, and the process by which peat is formed is studied in existing swamps in many parts of the world (e.g., in the Okefenokee Swamp of Georgia, U.S., and along the southwestern coast of New Guinea). The formation of peat is controlled by several factors including (1) the evolutionary development of plant life, (2) the climatic conditions (warm enough to sustain plant growth and wet enough to permit the partial decomposition of the plant material and preserve the peat), and (3) the physical conditions of the area (its geographic position relative to the sea or other bodies of water, rates of subsidence or uplift, and so forth). Warm moist climates are thought to produce broad bands of bright coal. Cooler temperate climates, on the other hand, are thought to produce detrital coal with relatively little bright coal.

Initially, the area on which a future coal seam may be developed must be uplifted so that plant growth can be established. Areas near seacoasts or low-lying areas near streams stay moist enough for peat to form, but elevated swamps (some bogs and moors) can produce peat only if the annual precipitation exceeds annual evaporation and little percolation or drainage occurs. Thick peat deposits necessary for coal formation develop at sites where the following conditions exist: slow, continuous subsidence; the presence of such natural structures as levees, beaches, and bars that give protection from frequent inundation; and a restricted supply of incoming sediments that would interrupt peat formation. In such areas the water may become quite stagnant (except for a few rivers traversing the swamp), and plant material can continue to accumulate. Microorganisms attack the plant material and convert it to peat.

Very close to the surface where oxygen is still readily available (aerobic, or oxidizing, conditions), the decomposition of the plant material produces mostly gaseous and liquid products. With increasing depth, however, the conditions become increasingly anaerobic (reducing), and molds and peats develop. The process of peat formation—biochemical coalification—is most active in the upper few metres of a peat deposit. Fungi are not found below about 0.5 metre (about 18 inches), and most forms of microbial life are eliminated at depths below about 10 metres (about 30 feet). If either the rate of subsidence or the rate of influx of new sediment increases, the peat will be buried and soon thereafter the coalification process—geochemical coalification—begins. The cycle may be repeated many times, which accounts for the numerous coal seams found in some sedimentary basins.

COALIFICATION

The general sequence of coalification is from lignite to subbituminous to bituminous to anthracite. Since microbial activity ceases within a few metres of the Earth's surface, the coalification process must be controlled primarily by changes in physical conditions that take place with depth. Some coal characteristics are determined by events that occur during peat formation—e.g., charcoal-like material in coal is attributed to fires that occurred during dry periods while peat was still forming.

Three major physical factors—duration, increasing temperature, and increasing pressure—may influence the coalification process. In laboratory experiments artificially prepared coals are influenced by the duration of the experiment, but in nature the length of time is substantially longer and the overall effect of time remains undetermined. Low-rank coal (i.e., brown coal) in the Moscow Basin was

BITUMINOUS COAL

Bituminous coal, also called soft coal, is the most abundant form of coal, intermediate in rank between subbituminous coal and anthracite according to the coal classification used in the United States and Canada. In Britain bituminous coal is commonly called "steam coal," and in Germany the term *Steinkohle* ("rock coal") is used. In the United States and Canada bituminous coal is divided into high-volatile, medium-volatile, and low-volatile bituminous groups. High-volatile bituminous coal is classified on the basis of its calorific value on a moist, ash-free basis (ranging from 24 to 33 megajoules per kg; 10,500 to 14,000 British thermal units per pound), while medium-volatile and low-volatile bituminous coals are classified on the basis of the percentage of fixed carbon present on a dry, ash-free basis (ranging from 69 to 78 percent for medium-volatile and from 78 to 86 percent for low-volatile bituminous coal). Medium-volatile and low-volatile bituminous coals typically have calorific values near 35 megajoules per kg (15,000 British thermal units per pound) on a dry, ash-free basis.

Bituminous coal is dark brown to black in colour and commonly banded, or layered. Because of its relatively high heat value and low (less than 3 percent) moisture content, its ease of transportation and storage, and its abundance, bituminous coal has the broadest range of commercial uses among the coals. It has long been utilized for steam generation in electric power plants and industrial boiler plants. In addition, bituminous coals that contain a fairly small amount of sulfur and cake (or "agglomerate") easily are the only coals suited for making metallurgical coke—a hard, spongelike substance of almost pure carbon important for smelting iron ore.

A major problem associated with the burning of bituminous coal is air pollution. Burning bituminous coal with a high sulfur content releases sulfur oxides into the air. Under certain conditions, nitrogen present in coal is also released in the form of nitrogen oxides. When moisture in the atmosphere reacts with these gases, acids such as sulfuric acid are produced and fall to Earth as wet acid deposition (acid rain)—an agent that can damage buildings and crops and cause water pollution. Because of these serious pollution problems, and regulations stemming from the 1990 Clean Air Act, a growing number of coal-fired electric power plants in the United States have either installed cleaning devices to reduce air pollution emissions or switched to low-sulfur subbituminous coal.

deposited during Carboniferous time but was not buried deeply and never reached a higher rank. The most widely accepted explanation is that coalification takes place in response to increasing temperature. In general, temperature increases with depth. This geothermal gradient averages about 30 °C (about 85 °F) per kilometre, but the gradient ranges from less than 10 °C (50 °F) per kilometre in regions undergoing very rapid subsidence to more than 100 °C (212 °F) per kilometre in areas of igneous activity. Measurements of thicknesses of sedimentary cover and corresponding coal ranks suggest that temperatures lower than 200 °C (about 390 °F) are sufficient to produce coal of anthracite rank. The effect of increasing pressure due to depth of burial is not considered to cause coalification. In fact, increasing overburden pressure might have the opposite effect if volatile compounds such as methane that must escape during coalification are retained. Pressure may influence the porosity and moisture content of coal.

HISTORY OF THE USE OF COAL

The discovery of the use of fire helped to distinguish humans from other animals. Early fuels were primarily wood (and charcoal derived from it), straw, and dried dung. References to the early uses of coal are meagre. Aristotle referred to "bodies which have more of earth than of smoke" and called them "coal-like substances."

(It should be noted that biblical references to coal are to charcoal rather than to the rock, coal.) Coal was used commercially by the Chinese long before it was utilized in Europe. Although no authentic record is available, coal from the Fushun mine in northeastern China may have been employed to smelt copper as early as 1000 BCE. Stones used as fuel were said to have been produced in China during the Han dynasty (206 BCE–220 CE).

Coal cinders found among Roman ruins in England suggest that the Romans were familiar with its use before 400 CE. The first documented proof that coal was mined in Europe was provided by the monk Reinier of Liège, who wrote (about 1200) of black earth very similar to charcoal used by metalworkers. Many references to coal mining in England, Scotland, and the European continent began to appear in the writings of the 13th century. Coal was, however, used only on a limited scale until the early 18th century, when Abraham Darby of England and others developed methods of using coke made from coal in blast furnaces and forges. Successive metallurgical and engineering developments—most notably the invention of the coal-burning steam engine by James Watt—engendered an almost insatiable demand for coal.

Up to the time of the American Revolution, most coal used in the American colonies came from England or Nova Scotia. Wartime shortages and the needs of the munitions manufacturers, however, spurred small American coal-mining operations such as those in Virginia on the James River near Richmond. By the early 1830s mining companies had emerged along the Ohio, Illinois, and Mississippi rivers and in the Appalachian region. As in European countries, the introduction of the steam locomotive gave the American coal industry a tremendous impetus. Continued expansion of industrial activity in the United States and in Europe further promoted the use of coal.

COKE

Coke is a solid residue remaining after certain types of bituminous coals are heated to a high temperature out of contact with air until substantially all of the volatile constituents have been driven off. The residue is chiefly carbon, with minor amounts of hydrogen, nitrogen, sulfur, and oxygen. Also present in coke is the mineral matter in the original coal, chemically altered and decomposed during the coking process.

Oven coke (size: 40 to 100 mm, about $1^1/_2$ to 4 inches) is used throughout the world in blast furnaces to make iron. Smaller quantities of coke are used in other metallurgical processes, such as the manufacture of ferroalloys, lead, and zinc, and in kilns to make lime and magnesia. Large, strong coke, known as foundry coke, is used in foundry cupolas to smelt iron ores. Smaller sizes of both oven and gas coke (15 to 50 mm) are used to heat houses and commercial buildings. Coke measuring 10 to 25 mm in size is employed in the manufacture of phosphorus and of calcium carbide, the raw material from which acetylene is made. Coke breeze (less than 12 mm) is applied to the sintering of small iron ore prior to use in blast furnaces. Any surplus breeze coke becomes industrial boiler fuel.

COAL RANK

As is noted above, the formation of coal from a variety of plant materials via biochemical and geochemical processes is called coalification. The nature of the constituents in coal is related to the degree of coalification, the measurement of which is termed rank. Rank is usually assessed by a series of tests, collectively called the proximate analysis, that determine the moisture content, volatile matter content, ash content, fixed-carbon content, and calorific value of a coal.

MOISTURE CONTENT

Moisture content is determined by heating an air-dried coal sample at 105–110 °C (221–230 °F) under specified conditions until a constant weight is obtained. In general, the moisture content increases with decreasing rank and ranges from 1 to 40 percent for the various ranks of coal. The presence of moisture is an important factor in both the storage and the utilization of coals, as it adds unnecessary weight during transportation, reduces the calorific value, and poses some handling problems.

VOLATILE MATTER CONTENT

Volatile matter is material that is driven off when coal is heated to 950 °C (1,742 °F) in the absence of air under specified conditions. It is measured practically by determining the loss of weight. Consisting of a mixture of gases, low-boiling-point organic compounds that condense into oils upon cooling, and tars, volatile matter increases with decreasing rank. In general, coals with high volatile-matter content ignite easily and are highly reactive in combustion applications.

MINERAL (ASH) CONTENT

Coal contains a variety of minerals in varying proportions that, when the coal is burned, are transformed into ash. The amount and nature of the ash and its behaviour at high temperatures affect the design and type of ash-handling system employed in coal-utilization plants. At high temperatures, coal ash becomes sticky (i.e., sinters) and eventually forms molten slag. The slag then becomes a hard, crystalline material upon cooling and resolidification.

A collection of ash from burnt coal. Assessing ash is one of the ways coal rank can be determined. Shutterstock.com

Specific ash-fusion temperatures are determined in the laboratory by observing the temperatures at which successive characteristic stages of fusion occur in a specimen of ash when heated in a furnace under specified conditions. These temperatures are often used as indicators of the clinkering potential of coals during high-temperature processing.

FIXED-CARBON CONTENT

Fixed carbon is the solid combustible residue that remains after a coal particle is heated and the volatile matter is expelled. The fixed-carbon content of a coal is determined by subtracting the percentages of moisture, volatile matter, and ash from a sample. Since gas-solid combustion reactions are slower than gas-gas reactions, a high fixed-carbon content indicates that the coal will require a long combustion time.

CALORIFIC VALUE

Calorific value, measured in British thermal units or megajoules per kilogram, is the amount of chemical energy stored in a coal that is released as thermal energy upon combustion. It is directly related to rank; in fact, the ASTM method uses calorific value to classify coals at or below the rank of high-volatile bituminous (above that rank, coals are classified by fixed-carbon content). The calorific value determines in part the value of a coal as a fuel for combustion applications.

In the United States and Canada, bituminous coal is divided into high-volatile, medium-volatile, and low-volatile bituminous groups. High-volatile bituminous coal is classified on the basis of its calorific value on a moist, ash-free basis (ranging from 24 to 33 megajoules per kg;

10,500 to 14,000 British thermal units per pound), while medium-volatile and low-volatile bituminous coals are classified on the basis of the percentage of fixed carbon present on a dry, ash-free basis (ranging from 69 to 78 percent for medium-volatile and from 78 to 86 percent for low-volatile bituminous coal). Medium-volatile and low-volatile bituminous coals typically have calorific values near 35 megajoules per kg (15,000 British thermal units per pound) on a dry, ash-free basis.

COAL TYPE

Coal is a complex material composed of microscopically distinguishable, physically distinctive, and chemically different organic substances called macerals. Based on their optical reflectance, mode of occurrence, and physical appearance under the microscope, macerals are grouped into three major classes: (1) Liptinite or exinite macerals, with low reflectance and high hydrogen-to-carbon ratios, are derived from plant spores, cuticles, resins, and algal bodies. (2) Vitrinite macerals, with intermediate reflectance and high oxygen-to-carbon ratios, are derived from woody tissues. (3) Inertinite macerals, with high reflectance and carbon contents, are derived from fossil charcoal or decayed material.

Although the various macerals in a given group are expected to have similar properties, they often exhibit different behaviour in a particular end use. For example, combustion efficiency is reported to be inversely related to inertinite content, yet micrinite, which is classified as an inertinite maceral, is found to be highly reactive in combustion applications. Correlations between petrographic composition and coal reactivity have not yet been well established.

CHAPTER 6
OBTAINING COAL

A s is the case with petroleum and natural gas, the find-ing of usable deposits of coal and their extraction from below the surface of the Earth involves the skills of geologists and engineers.

WORLD DISTRIBUTION OF COAL

Coal deposits are known to have formed more than 400 million years ago. Most anthracite and bituminous coals occur within the 299- to 359.2-million-year-old strata of the Carboniferous Period, the so-called first coal age. The formation of coal deposits continued through the Permian, Triassic, and Jurassic periods into the "second coal age," which includes the Cretaceous, Paleogene, and Neogene periods. Coals of the Cretaceous Period (145.5 million to 65.5 million years ago) are generally in the high-volatile to medium-volatile bituminous ranks. Cenozoic coals, formed less than 65.5 million years ago, are predomi-nantly of the subbituminous and lignitic ranks.

GENERAL OCCURRENCE

Coal is a widespread resource of energy and chemicals. Although terrestrial plants necessary for the development of coal did not become abundant until Carboniferous time, large sedimentary basins containing Carboniferous and younger rocks are known on virtually every continent, including Antarctica. The presence of large coal deposits

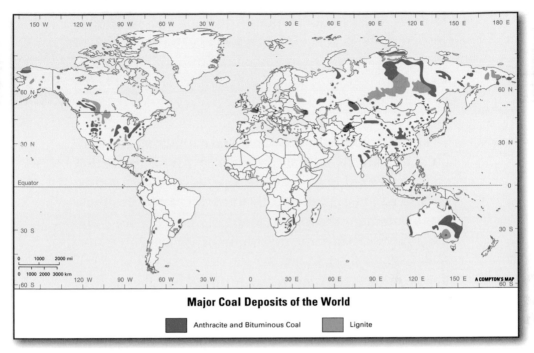

Major Coal Deposits of the World

Anthracite and Bituminous Coal   Lignite

in regions that now have arctic or subarctic climates (such as Alaska and Siberia) is due to climatic changes and to the tectonic motion of crustal plates that moved ancient continental masses over the Earth's surface, sometimes through subtropical and even tropical regions.

The absence of coal in some areas (such as Greenland and much of northern Canada) results from the fact that the rocks found there are older than Carboniferous period and that these regions, known as shields, lacked the abundant terrestrial plant life needed for the formation of major coal deposits.

RESOURCES AND RESERVES

World coal reserves and resources are difficult to assess. Although some of the difficulty stems from the lack of accurate data for individual countries, two fundamental problems make these estimates difficult and subjective. The first problem concerns differences in the definition of terms such as *proven reserves* (generally only those quantities that are recoverable) and *geological resources* (generally the total amount of coal present, whether or not recoverable at present).

The proven reserves for any commodity should provide a reasonably accurate estimate of the amount that can be recovered under existing operating and economic conditions. To be economically mineable, a coal bed must have a minimum thickness (about 0.6 metre; 2 feet) and be buried less than some maximum depth (roughly 2,000 metres; 6,600 feet) below the Earth's surface. These values of thickness and depth are not fixed but change with coal quality, demand, the ease with which overlying rocks can be removed (in surface mining) or a shaft sunk to reach the coal seam (in underground mining), and so forth. The development of new mining techniques may increase the amount of coal that can be extracted relative to the amount that cannot be removed. For example, in underground mining (which accounts for about 60 percent of world coal production), conventional mining methods leave behind large pillars of coal to support the overlying rocks and recover only about half of the coal present. On the other hand, longwall mining, in which the equipment removes continuous parallel bands of coal, may recover nearly all the coal present.

The second problem, which concerns the estimation of reserves, is the rate at which a commodity is consumed. When considering the worldwide reserves of coal, the number of years that coal will be available may be more important than the total amount of coal resources. At present rates of consumption, world coal reserves should last more than 300–500 years. A large amount of additional

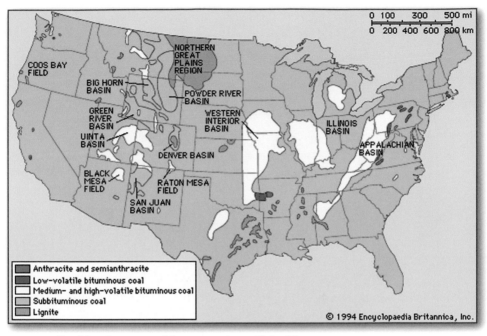

Coal-bearing areas of the conterminous United States.

coal is present in the Earth but cannot be recovered at this time. These resources, sometimes called "geologic resources," are even more difficult to estimate, but they are thought to be as much as 15 times greater than the amount of proven reserves.

One ton of coal equivalent equals 1 metric ton (2,205 pounds) of coal with a heating value of 29.3 megajoules per kg (12,600 British thermal units per pound). These values suggest that the United States has the largest amount of recoverable coal. Nearly 80 percent of the world's recoverable coal resources are controlled by seven countries: the United States (about 27 percent), Russia (about 17 percent), China (about 13 percent), India (about 10 percent), South Africa (about 5 percent), Ukraine (about 4 percent), and Kazakhstan (about 3 percent)

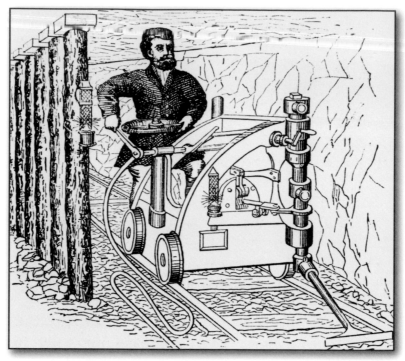

Rail-mounted coal-cutting machine, used in underground mining during the 19th century. © Photos.com/Jupiterimages

COAL MINING

The various methods of mining a coal seam can be classified under two headings, surface mining and underground mining. Surface and underground coal mining are broad activities that incorporate numerous variations in equipment and methods, and the choice of which method to use in extracting a coal seam depends on many technological, economic, and social factors.

The technological factors include, at a minimum, the number of seams, the thickness and steepness of each seam, the nature and thickness of the strata overlying the seams, the quality of the coal seams, the surface topography, the surface features, and the transportation networks available. Economic factors include energy demand and its growth, the supply and cost of alternative sources of energy, coal quality and the cost of coal preparation, the selling price of coal, advancements in technology that affect costs of production, and environmental legislation. Social factors include prior history of mining in the area, ownership patterns, availability of labour, and local or regional government support.

It is a general rule that technological factors dictate a clear choice between surface and underground mining, whereas economic and social factors determine whether a coal reserve will be mined at all. Some coal reserves, however, are surface-mined first and then deep-mined when the coal seam extends to such great depths that it becomes uneconomical to continue with surface mining.

Analysis of world coal production indicates that contributions from surface and underground production are approximately equal. Anthracite seams (less than 10 percent of world coal production) are generally mined by underground methods, whereas lignite seams (25 percent) are most often surface-mined. Bituminous seams (approximately 65 percent) are mined in roughly equal proportions by both methods.

SURFACE MINING

Surface coal mining generally involves the following sequence of unit operations: (1) clearing the land of trees and vegetation, (2) removing and storing the top layers of the unconsolidated soil (topsoil), (3) drilling the hard strata over the coal seam, (4) fragmenting or blasting the hard strata with explosives, (5) removing the blasted material, exposing the coal seam, and cleaning the top of the coal seam, (6) fragmenting the coal seam, as required, by drilling and blasting, (7) loading the loose coal onto haulage conveyances, (8) transporting the coal from the mine to the plant, and (9) reclaiming lands affected by the mining activity.

Surface techniques can be broadly classified into (1) contour strip mining, (2) area strip mining, (3) open-pit mining, and (4) auger mining.

Contour mining is commonly practiced where a coal seam outcrops in rolling or hilly terrain. Basically, the method consists of removing the overburden above the coal seam and then, starting at the outcrop and proceeding along the hillside, creating a bench around the hill. In the past, the blasted overburden spoil was simply shoved down the hill; currently, soil is either carried down the mountain to fill a chosen valley in horizontal layers or is replaced on the working bench itself in places where coal has been removed. If the break-even stripping ratio remains favourable, further cuts into the hillside will be made. Otherwise, if there are sufficient reserves under the knob of the hill, the coal may be recovered by underground mining or by augering.

Area mining, applied where the terrain is flat, commences with a trench or "box cut" made through the overburden to expose a portion of the coal seam. This trench is extended to the limits of the property in the strike direction. After coal removal, a second cut is made parallel to the first one, and the overburden material from this cut is placed in the void of the first cut. The process is repeated in successive parallel cuts until the stripping ratio indicates that continued surface mining is uneconomical.

In open-pit mining of the coal seam, several benches are established in both the overburden strata and the coal seam. The open-pit method is generally practiced where thick coal seams are overlain by thick or thin overburden; it is also used for mining steeply pitching coal seams. In the beginning stages of mining, considerable volumes of overburden materials must be accumulated in large dump areas outside the mine.

Auger mining is usually associated with contour strip mining. With this method, the coal is removed by drilling auger holes from the last contour cut and extracting it in the same manner that shavings are produced by a carpenter's bit. Coal recovery rates approach 60 percent with this method. The cutting heads of some augers are as high as 2.5 metres (8 feet). As each stem works its way into the coal seam, additional auger stems are added, so that hole depths of more than 60 to 100 metres (200 to 330 feet) are not uncommon. Problems of subsidence, water pollution, and potential fires are associated with augering.

Highwall mining is an adaptation of auger mining. Instead of an auger hole, an entry into the coal seam is made by a continuous miner, remotely operated from a cabin at the surface. The cut coal is transported by conveyors behind the miner to the outside. Using a television camera, the operator can see and control the miner's progress. The entry can be advanced 300 to 400 metres (1,000 to 1,300 feet) into the coal seam, after which the miner is retreated to the surface and repositioned to drive an entry adjacent to the previous one. Advantages over augering include higher productivity, greater safety, and lower cost.

UNDERGROUND MINING

In underground coal mining, the working environment is completely enclosed by the geologic medium, which consists of the coal seam and the overlying and underlying strata. Access to the coal seam is gained by suitable openings from the surface, and a network of roadways driven in the seam then facilitates the installation of service facilities for such essential activities as human and material transport, ventilation, water handling and drainage, and

MINE GAS

Mine gas is any of various harmful vapours produced during mining operations. To help coal miners avoid the perils of gas buildup, ventilation of underground mines is extremely important, and has been for ages.

Three methods of ventilating a mine, woodcut from De re metallica by Georgius Agricola, published 1556. The Granger Collection, New York

The gases are frequently called damps (German *Dampf*, "vapour"). Firedamp is a gas that occurs naturally in coal seams. The gas is nearly always methane (CH_4) and is highly inflammable and explosive when present in the air in a proportion of 5 to 14 percent. White damp, or carbon monoxide (CO), is a particularly toxic gas; as little as 0.1 percent can cause death within a few minutes. It is a product of the incomplete combustion of carbon and is formed in coal mines chiefly by the oxidation of coal, particularly in those mines where spontaneous combustion occurs. Black damp is an atmosphere in which a flame lamp will not burn, usually because of an excess of carbon dioxide (CO_2) and nitrogen in the air. Stinkdamp is the name given by miners to hydrogen sulfide (H_2S) because of its characteristic smell of rotten eggs. Afterdamp is the mixture of gases found in a mine after an explosion or fire.

power. This phase of an underground mining operation is termed "mine development." Often the extraction of coal from the seam during mine development is called "first mining"; the extraction of the remaining seam is called "second mining."

Modern underground coal-mining methods can be classified into four distinct categories: room-and-pillar, longwall, shortwall, and thick-seam.

ROOM-AND-PILLAR MINING

In this method, a number of parallel entries are driven into the coal seam. The entries are connected at intervals by wider entries, called rooms, that are cut through the seam at right angles to the entries. The resulting grid formation creates thick pillars of coal that support the overhead strata of earth and rock. There are two main room-and-pillar systems, the conventional and the continuous. In the conventional system, the unit operations of undercutting, drilling, blasting, and loading are performed by separate machines and work crews. In a continuous operation, one machine—the continuous miner—rips coal from the face and loads it directly into a hauling unit. In both methods, the exposed roof is supported after loading, usually by rock bolts.

Under favourable conditions, between 30 and 50 percent of the coal in an area can be recovered during development of the pillars. For recovering coal from the pillars themselves, many methods are practiced, depending on the roof and floor conditions. The increased pressure created by pillar removal must be transferred in an orderly manner to the remaining pillars, so that there is no excessive accumulation of stress on them. Otherwise, the unrecovered pillars may start to fail, endangering the miners and mining equipment. The general procedure is to extract one row of pillars at a time, leaving the mined-out portion, or gob, free to subside. While extraction of all the coal in a pillar is a desirable objective, partial pillar extraction schemes are more common.

At depths greater than 400 to 500 metres (1,300 to 1,650 feet), room-and-pillar methods become very difficult to practice, owing to excessive roof pressure and the larger pillar sizes that are required.

Longwall Mining

In the longwall mining method, mine development is carried out in such a manner that large blocks of coal, usually 100 to 300 metres wide and 1,000 to 3,000 metres long (330 to 1,000 feet wide and 3,300 to 10,000 feet long), are available for complete extraction. A block of coal is extracted in slices, the dimensions of which are fixed by the height of coal extracted, the width of the longwall

A longwall miner shearing coal at the face of a coal seam; from an underground mine in southern Ohio, U.S. Joy Technologies Inc.

face, and the thickness of the slice (ranging from 0.6 to 1.2 metres [2 to 4 feet]). In manual or semimechanized operations, the coal is undercut along the width of the panel to the depth of the intended slice. It is then drilled and blasted, and the broken coal is loaded onto a conveyor at the face. The sequence of operations continues with support of the roof at the face and shifting of the conveyor forward. The cycle of cutting, drilling, blasting, loading, roof supporting, and conveyor shifting is repeated until the entire block is mined out.

In modern mechanized longwall operations, the coal is cut and loaded onto a face conveyor by continuous longwall miners called shearers or plows. The roof is supported by mechanized, self-advancing supports called longwall shields, which form a protective steel canopy under which the face conveyor, workers, and shearer operate. In combination with shields and conveyors, longwall shearers or plows create a truly continuous mining system with a huge production capacity. Record productions exceeding 20,000 tons per day, 400,000 tons per month, and 3.5 million tons per year have been reported from a single U.S. longwall shearer face.

Two main longwall systems are widely practiced. The system described above, known as the retreating method, is the most commonly used in the United States. In this method the block is developed to its boundary first, and then the block is mined back toward the main haulage tunnel. In the advancing longwall method, which is more common in Europe, development of the block takes place only 30 to 40 metres (100 to 130 feet) ahead of the mining of the block, and the two operations proceed together to the boundary.

In longwall mining, as in the room-and-pillar system, the safe transfer of roof pressures to the solid coal ahead of the face and to the caved roof behind the face is necessary. Caving of the overlying strata generally extends to the surface, causing surface subsidence. The subsid ence over a longwall face is generally more uniform than it is over room-and-pillar workings. If conditions are such that the roof will not cave or subsidence to the surface is not allowable, it will be necessary to backfill the void with materials such as sand, waste from coal-preparation plants, or fly ash. Owing to technical and environmental reasons, backfilling is practiced in many mining countries (e.g., Poland, India), but the cost of production is much higher with backfilling than it is without.

SHORTWALL MINING

In the shortwall mining method, the layout is similar to the longwall method except that the block of coal is not more than 100 metres (330 feet) wide. Furthermore, the slices are as much as three metres thick and are taken by a continuous miner. The mined coal is dumped onto a face conveyor or other face haulage equipment. The roof is supported by specially designed shields, which operate in the same manner as longwall shields. Although a great future was envisioned for shortwall mining, it has not lived up to expectations.

THICK-SEAM MINING

Coal seams as much as 5 metres (16.5 feet) thick can be mined in a single "lift" by the longwall method, and seams up to 7 metres (23 feet) thick have been extracted by con-ventional mining systems in one pass. However, when a seam exceeds these thicknesses, its extraction usually involves dividing the seam into a number of slices and min-ing each slice with longwall, continuous, or conventional mining methods. The thickness of each slice may vary from 3 to 4 metres (10 to 13 feet). Many variations exist in the manner in which the complete seam is extracted. The slices may be taken in ascending or descending order. If the roof conditions or spontaneous-combustion liability of the seam requires that there be no caving, the void created by mining will be backfilled. The backfill material then acts as an artificial floor or roof for the next slice. Caving is the preferred practice, however.

Thick coal seams containing soft coal or friable bands and overlain by a medium-to-strong roof that parts easily from the coal can be fragmented by a high-pressure water jet. For successful operation, the floor must not deteriorate through contact with water, and the seam gradient must be steep enough to allow the water to flush the broken coal from the mined areas. Under favourable conditions, hydraulic mining of coal is productive, safe, and economical. It has been employed experimentally within the United States and Canada, but it is practiced extensively in the Kuznetsk Basin of Siberia for the extraction of multiseam, steeply pitching deposits. Here the water is also used to transport the coal from the working faces to a common point through open channels and from the common point to the surface through high-pressure hydraulic transportation systems.

CHAPTER 7
UTILIZATION
OF COAL

Coal finds most of its use in combustion or in conversion into useful solid, gaseous, and liquid products. By far the most important use of coal is in combustion, mainly to provide heat to the boilers of electric power plants. Metallurgical coke is the major product of coal conversion. In addition, techniques for gasifying and liquefying coal into fuels or into feedstocks for the chemical industry are well developed, but their commercial viability depends on the availability and price of the competing fossil fuels, petroleum and natural gas.

COMBUSTION

The most common and important use of coal is in combustion, in which heat is generated to produce steam, which in turn powers the turbines that produce electricity. Combustion for electricity generation by utilities is the end use for 86 percent of the coal mined in the United States.

COMBUSTION REACTIONS

The main chemical reactions that contribute to heat release are oxidation reactions, which convert the constituent elements of coal into their respective oxides. In the table, the negative signs indicate reactions that release heat (exothermic reactions), whereas the positive sign indicates a reaction that absorbs heat (endothermic reaction).

PRINCIPAL OXIDATION REACTIONS IN THE COMBUSTION OF COAL	
REACTION	CHANGE IN HEAT (IN BRITISH THERMAL UNITS PER POUND-MOLE)
carbon + oxygen = carbon dioxide	-169,293
hydrogen + oxygen = water	-122,971
sulfur + oxygen = sulfur dioxide	-127,728
nitrogen + oxygen = nitrogen monoxide	+77,760

The combustion of a coal particle occurs primarily in two stages: (1) evolution of volatile matter during the initial stages of heating, with accompanying physical and chemical changes, and (2) subsequent combustion of the residual char. Following ignition and combustion of the evolving volatile matter, oxygen diffuses to the surface of the particle and ignites the char. In some instances, ignition of volatile matter and char occurs simultaneously. The steps involved in char oxidation are as follows:

1. Diffusion of oxygen from the bulk gas to the char surface
2. Reaction between oxygen and the surface of the char particle
3. Diffusion of reaction products from the surface of the char particle into the bulk gas

At low combustion temperatures, the rate of the chemical reaction (step 2) determines (or limits) the overall reaction rate. However, since the rate of a chemical reaction increases exponentially with temperature, the carbon-oxygen reaction (step 2) can become so fast at high temperatures that the diffusion of oxygen to the surface (step 1) can no longer keep up. In this case, the overall reaction rate is controlled or limited by the diffusion rate of oxygen to the reacting char surface. The controlling mechanism of the combustion reaction therefore depends on such parameters as particle size, reaction temperature, and inherent reactivity of the coal particle.

FIXED-BED COMBUSTION

In fixed-bed systems, lumps of coal, usually size-graded between 3 and 50 mm, are heaped onto a grate, and preheated primary air (called underfire air) is blown from under the bed to burn the fixed carbon. Some secondary air (overfire air) is introduced over the coal bed to burn the volatiles released from the bed. Based on the method of feeding the coal, these systems can be further classified into underfeed, overfeed, spreader, and traveling-grate stoker methods.

The coking characteristics of a coal can influence its combustion behaviour by forming clinkers of coke and ash and thus resisting proper air distribution through the bed. Fines in the coal feed can also cause uneven distribution of air, but this problem can be reduced by adding some water to the feed coal. This procedure, known as tempering, reduces resistance to airflow by agglomerating the fines.

The relatively large coal feed size used in fixed-bed systems limits the rate of heating of the particles to about 1 °C (1.8 °F) per second, thereby establishing the time required for combustion of the particles at about 45 to 60 minutes. In addition, the sizes of the grates in these systems impose an upper limit on a fixed-bed combustor of about 100,000 megajoules (10^8 British thermal units) per hour. Therefore, this type of system is limited to industrial and small-scale power plants.

FLUIDIZED-BED COMBUSTION

In fluidized-bed combustion, a bed of crushed solid particles (usually six mm or less) is made to behave like a fluid by an airstream passing from the bottom of the bed at sufficient velocity to suspend the material in it. The bed material—usually a mixture of coal and sand, ash, or limestone—possesses many of the properties of, and behaves like, a fluid. Crushed coal is introduced into the bubbling bed, which is usually preheated to about 850–950 °C (1,562–1,742 °F). Coal particles are heated at approximately 1,000 °C (1,800 °F) per second and are devolatilized, and the residual char is burned in about 20 minutes. Coal concentration in the bed is maintained between 1 and 5 percent by weight. Since the bed is continuously bubbling and mixing like a boiling liquid, transfer of heat to and from the bed is very efficient and, hence, uniform temperatures can be achieved throughout the bed. Because of this efficient heat transfer, less surface area is required to remove heat from the bed (and raise steam); therefore, there are lower total capital costs associated with a given heat load. Also, lower combustion temperatures reduce the fouling and corrosion of heat-transfer surfaces. (Fouling is the phenomenon of coal ash sticking to surfaces.) Ash from a fluidized-bed combustion system is amorphous—that is, it has not undergone melting and resolidification.

Fluidized-bed combustion systems are particularly suitable for coals of low quality and high sulfur content because of their capacity to retain sulfur dioxide (SO_2; a pollutant gas) within the bed and their ability to burn coals of high or variable ash content. When limestone (calcium

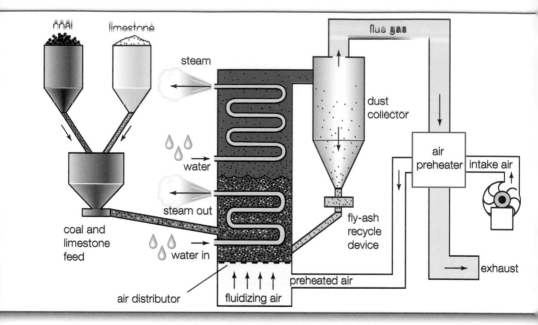

Schematic diagram of a fluidized-bed combustion boiler. Encyclopædia Britannica, Inc.

carbonate; $CaCO_3$) or dolomite (a mixture of calcium and magnesium carbonates; $CaMg(CO_3)_2$) is introduced into the bed along with the coal, the limestone decomposes to calcium oxide (CaO), which then reacts in the bed with most of the SO_2 released from the burning coal to produce calcium sulfate ($CaSO_4$). The $CaSO_4$ can be removed as a solid by-product for use in a variety of applications. In addition, partially spent calcium or magnesium can be regenerated and recycled by a variety of techniques. The formation and emission of nitrogen oxides (NOx; another pollutant gas) are inhibited by low operating temperatures. Fluidized-bed combustors, in general, need additional equipment (such as cyclone separators) to separate fines containing a high amount of combustibles and recycle them back into the system.

PULVERIZED-COAL COMBUSTION

Pulverized-coal combustion is widely used in large power stations because it offers flexible control. In this method, coal is finely ground so that 70 to 80 percent by weight passes through a 200-mesh screen. The powder is burned in a combustion chamber by entraining the particles in combustion air. Because finely ground coal has more surface area per unit weight than larger particles, the combustion reactions occur at a faster rate, thus reducing the time required for complete combustion to about 1 to 2 seconds. The high heating rates associated with fine particles, coupled with the high combustion temperatures (about 1,700 °C, or 3,092 °F) and short burning times, lead to high throughputs.

By carefully designing the combustion chamber, a wide variety of coals—ranging from lignites to anthracites and including high-ash coals—can be burned at high combustion efficiencies. Depending on the characteristics of the mineral content, combustion furnaces are designed to remove ash as either a dry powder or a liquid slag. Furnaces used for pulverized coal are classified according to the firing method as vertical, horizontal, or tangential.

The disadvantages of this mode of combustion are the relatively high costs associated with drying and grinding coal, the fouling and slagging of heat-transfer surfaces, and the need for expensive fine-particle-collection equipment.

CYCLONE COMBUSTION

In a cyclone furnace, small coal particles (less than six mm) are burned while entrained in air. The stream of coal particles in the primary combustion air enters tangentially into a cylindrical chamber, where it meets a high-speed tangential stream of secondary air. Owing to the intense mixing of fuel and air, the temperatures developed inside the furnace are high (up to 2,150 °C, or 3,900 °F). At such high temperatures, the rate of the overall reaction is governed by the rate of transfer of oxygen to the particle surface, and the availability of oxygen is increased by the high turbulence induced in the combustion chamber. Combustion intensities and efficiencies are therefore high in cyclone combustors. As a result of the high temperatures, ash melts and flows along the inclined wall of the furnace and is removed as a liquid slag.

Coal-Water Slurry Fuel

Pulverized coal can be mixed with water and made into a slurry, which can be handled like a liquid fuel and burned in a boiler designed to burn oil. Coal-water slurry fuel (CWSF) normally consists of 50–70 percent pulverized or micronized coal, 29–49 percent water, and less than 1 percent chemicals to disperse the coal particles in the water and prevent settling of the coal. The slurry is finely sprayed (atomized) into a combustion chamber in a manner similar to that used for fuel oil.

However, the challenge in combustion of CWSF is to achieve quick evaporation of the water from the droplets in order to facilitate ignition and combustion of the coal particles within the available residence time. This can be achieved by ensuring very fine atomization of the CWSF, using preheated combustion air, and providing good recirculation of hot combustion-product gases in the flame zone. Heat loss owing to evaporation of water imposes some penalty on the thermal efficiency of the boiler, but this may represent less of a cost than the dewatering of wet coal or the capital costs involved in converting an oil-fired

When crushed and mixed with water, coal becomes a tarry-looking liquid called slurry, which itself can be used as an energy source. Steve Liss/Time & Life Pictures/Getty Images

combustor into a dry-coal-fired unit. The commercial viability of CWSF depends on the price and availability of
naturally occurring liquid fuels.

ADVANCED COMBUSTION TECHNOLOGIES

The burning of coal can produce combustion gases as hot
as 2,500 °C (4,500 °F), but the lack of materials that can
withstand such heat forces even modern power plants to
limit steam temperatures to about 540 °C (1,000 °F)—even
though the thermal efficiency of a power plant increases
with increasing operating fluid (steam) temperature. An
advanced combustion system called magnetohydrody-
namics (MHD) uses coal to generate a high-temperature
combustion gas at about 2,480 °C (4,500 °F). At this temperature, gas molecules are ionized (electrically charged).
A part of the energy in the product stream is converted
directly into electrical energy by passing the charged gases
through a magnetic field, and the partially cooled gases are
then passed through a conventional steam generator. This
process enhances the overall thermal efficiency of energy
conversion to about 50 percent—as opposed to conventional processes, which have an efficiency of about 36 to
38 percent.

Another advanced method of utilizing coal, known
as the Integrated Gasification Combined Cycle, involves
gasifying the coal (described below) and burning the gas
to produce hot products of combustion at 1,600 °C (2,900
°F). These gaseous products in turn run a gas turbine, and
the exhaust gases from the gas turbine can then be used to
generate steam to run a conventional steam turbine. Such
a combined-cycle operation involving both gas and steam
turbines can improve the overall efficiency of energy conversion to about 42 percent.

GASIFICATION

While the goal of combustion is to produce the maximum amount of heat possible by oxidizing all the combustible material, the goal of gasification is to convert most of the combustible solids into combustible gases such as carbon monoxide, hydrogen, and methane.

GASIFICATION REACTIONS

During gasification, coal initially undergoes devolatilization, and the residual char undergoes some or all of a number of reactions. The table also shows qualitatively the thermodynamic, kinetic, and equilibrium considerations of the reactions. As indicated by the heats of reaction, the combustion reactions are exothermic (and fast), whereas some of the gasification reactions are endothermic (and slower). Usually, the heat required to induce the endothermic gasification reactions is provided by combustion or partial combustion of some of the coal. Gasification reactions are particularly sensitive to the temperature and pressure in the system. High temperature and low pressure are suitable for the formation of most of the gasification products, except methane; methane formation if favoured by low temperatures and high pressures.

For thermodynamic and kinetic considerations, char is taken to be graphite, or pure carbon. In reality, however, coal char is a mixture of pure carbon and impurities with structural defects. Because impurities and defects can be catalytic in nature, the absolute reaction rate depends on their amount and nature—and also on such physical characteristics as surface area and pore structure, which control the accessibility of reactants to the surface. These characteristics in turn depend on

COAL GASIFICATION REACTIONS

REACTION	EQUILIBRIUM CONDITIONS		KINETICS (RATE OF REACTION)	HEAT OF REACTION
	EFFECT OF INCREASE IN TEMPERATURE	EFFECT OF INCREASE IN PRESSURE		
SOLID-GAS				
carbon + oxygen = carbon monoxide (partial combustion)	to right	to left	fast	exothermic
carbon + oxygen = carbon dioxide (combustion)	—	—	very fast	exothermic
carbon + carbon dioxide = carbon monoxide (Boudward)	to right	to left	slow	endothermic
carbon + water = carbon monoxide + hydrogen (water-gas)	to right	to left	moderate	endothermic
carbon + hydrogen = methane (hydrogasification)	to left	to right	slow	exothermic
GAS-GAS				
carbon monoxide + water = carbon dioxide + hydrogen (shift)	to left	—	moderate	exothermic
carbon monoxide + hydrogen = methane + water	to left	to right	slow	exothermic

Maintaining a gasifier. Through superheating gasifiers convert carbon-based fuel sources, such as coal, to high-grade synthetic fuels. Phillip Spears/ Photodisc/Getty Images

the nature of the parent coal and on the devolatilization conditions.

GASIFICATION SYSTEMS

The operating temperature of a gasifier usually dictates the nature of the ash-removal system. Operating temperatures below 1,000 °C (1,800 °F) allow dry ash removal, whereas temperatures between 1,000 and 1,200 °C (1,800 and 2,200 °F) cause the ash to melt partially and form agglomerates. Temperatures above 1,200 °C result in melting of the ash, which is removed mostly in the form of liquid slag. Gasifiers may operate at either atmospheric or elevated pressure; both temperature and pressure affect the composition of the final product gases.

Gasification processes use one or a combination of three reactant gases: oxygen (O_2), steam (H_2O), and hydrogen (H_2). The heat required for the endothermic gasification reactions is suppled by the exothermic combustion reactions between the coal and oxygen. Air can be used to produce a gaseous mixture of nitrogen (N_2), carbon monoxide (CO), and carbon dioxide (CO_2), with low calorific value (about 6 to 12 megajoules per cubic metre, or 150–300 British thermal units per cubic foot). Oxygen can be used to produce a mixture of carbon monoxide, hydrogen, and some noncombustible gases, with medium calorific value (12 to 16 megajoules per cubic metre, or 300 to 400 British thermal units per cubic foot). Hydrogasification processes use hydrogen to produce a gas (mainly methane, CH_4) of high calorific value (37 to 41 megajoules per cubic metre, or 980 to 1,080 British thermal units per cubic foot).

Methods of contacting the solid feed and the gaseous reactants in a gasifier are of four main types: fixed bed, fluidized bed, entrained flow, and molten bath. The operating principles of the first three systems are similar to those discussed above for combustion systems. The molten-bath approach is similar to the fluidized-bed concept in that reactions take place in a molten medium (either slag or salt) that disperses the coal and acts as a heat sink for distributing the heat of combustion.

THE LURGI SYSTEM

The most important fixed-bed gasifier available commercially is the Lurgi gasifier, developed by the Lurgi Company in Germany in the 1930s. It is a dry-bottom, fixed-bed system usually operated at pressures between 30 and 35 atmospheres. Since it is a pressurized system, coarse-sized coal (25 to 45 mm) is fed into the gasifier through a lock hopper from the top. The gasifying medium (a steam-oxygen mixture) is introduced through a grate located in the bottom of the gasifier. The coal charge and the gasifying medium move in opposite directions, or countercurrently. At the operating temperature of about 980 °C (1,800 °F), the oxygen reacts with coal to form carbon dioxide, thereby producing heat to sustain the endothermic steam-carbon and carbon dioxide-carbon reactions. The raw product gas, consisting mainly of carbon monoxide, hydrogen, and methane, leaves the gasifier for further clean-up.

Besides participating in the gasification reactions, steam prevents high temperatures at the bottom of the gasifier so as not to sinter or melt the ash. Thus, the Lurgi system is most suitable for highly reactive coals. Large commercial gasifiers are capable of gasifying about 50 tons of coal per hour.

THE WINKLER SYSTEM

The Winkler gasifier is a fluidized-bed gasification system that operates at atmospheric pressure. In this gasifier, coal (usually crushed to less than 12 mm) is fed by a screw feeder and is fluidized by the gasifying medium (steam-air or steam-oxygen, depending on the declared calorific value of the product gas) entering through a grate at the bottom. The coal charge and the gasification medium move cocurrently (in the same direction). In addition to the main gasification reactions taking place in the bed, some may also take place in the freeboard above the bed. The temperature of the bed is usually maintained at 980 °C (1,800 °F), and the product gas consists primarily of carbon monoxide and hydrogen.

The low operating temperature and pressure of the Winkler system limits the throughput of the gasifier. Because of the low operating temperatures, lignites and subbituminous coals, which have high ash-fusion temperatures, are ideal feedstocks. Units capable of gasifying 40 to 45 tons per hour are commercially available.

THE KOPPERS-TOTZEK SYSTEM

The Koppers-Totzek gasifier has been the most successful entrained-flow gasifier. This process uses pulverized coal (usually less than 74 micrometres) blown into the gasifier by a mixture of steam and oxygen. The gasifier is operated at atmospheric pressure and at high temperatures of about 1,600–1,900 °C (2,900–3,450 °F). The coal dust and gasification medium flow cocurrently in the gasifier, and, because of the small coal-particle size, the residence time of the particle in the gasifier is approximately one second. Although this residence time is relatively short, high temperatures enhance the reaction rates, and therefore almost any coal can be gasified in the Koppers-Totzek system. Tars and oils are evolved at moderate temperatures but crack at higher temperatures, so that there is no condensible tarry material in the products. The ash melts and flows as slag. The product gas, known as synthesis gas (a mixture of carbon monoxide and hydrogen), is primarily used for ammonia manufacture.

ADVANCED GASIFICATION SYSTEMS

Many attempts have been made to improve the first-generation commercial gasifiers described above. The improvements are primarily aimed at increasing operating pressures in order to increase the throughput or at increasing operating temperatures in order to accommodate a variety of coal feeds. For example, British Gas Corporation converted the Lurgi gasifier from a dry-bottom to a slagging type by increasing the operating temperature. This allows the system to accommodate higher-rank coals that require higher temperatures for complete gasification.

COAL GAS

Coal gas is a flammable gaseous mixture—mainly hydrogen, methane, and carbon monoxide—formed by the destructive distillation (i.e., heating in the absence of air) of bituminous coal during the making of coke. Sometimes steam is added to react with the hot coke, thus increasing the yield of gas.

Coal gas represented one of the first major advances in lighting at the beginning of the industrial age. Coal gas was first made in the 1690s by heating coal in the presence of water to yield methane, and in 1792 William Murdock developed the gas jet lighting fixture. The first large building to have gas lighting (from a small gas plant on the site) was James Watt's foundry in Birmingham, Eng., in 1803. The Gas Light and Coke Company was founded in London in 1812 as the first real public utility, producing coal gas as a part of the coking process in large central plants and distributing it through underground pipes to individual users; soon many major cities had gasworks and distribution networks. Gas was expensive, however, and was used mainly for lighting, not for heating or cooking; it also contained many impurities that produced undesirable products of combustion (particularly carbon soot) in occupied spaces. Relatively pure methane in the form of natural gas would not be available until the exploitation of large oil fields in the 20th century.

Another version of the Lurgi gasifier is the Ruhr-100 process, with operating pressures about three times those of the basic Lurgi process. Developmental work on the Winkler process led to the pressurized Winkler process, which aimed at increasing the yield of methane in order to produce synthetic natural gas (SNG).

The Texaco gasifier (acquired by GE Energy in 2004) is a particularly promising new entrained-bed gasification system. In this system, coal is fed into the gasifier in the form of coal-water slurry; the water in the slurry serves as

both a transport medium (in liquid form) and a gasification medium (as steam). This system operates at 1,500 °C
(2,700 °F), so that the ash is removed as molten slag.

GAS-CLEANUP SYSTEMS

The product gas leaving a gasifier sometimes needs to be
cleaned of particulate matter, liquid by-products, sulfur
compounds, and oxides of carbon. Particulate matter is
conventionally removed from the raw gas with cyclones,
scrubbers, baghouses, or electrostatic precipitators.
Acidic gases such as hydrogen sulfide (H_2S) and carbon
dioxide are absorbed by various solvents such as amines
and carbonates. Since most gas-cleanup systems operate at
only moderate temperatures, the raw gases from a gasifier
have to be cooled before processing and then reheated if
necessary before end use. This reduces the overall thermal
efficiency of the process. For this reason, there is considerable interest in the development of hot gas-cleanup
systems capable of cleaning raw gas at high temperatures
with high efficiencies.

LIQUEFACTION

Liquefaction is the process of converting solid coal into
liquid fuels. The main difference between naturally occurring petroleum fuels and coal is the deficiency of hydrogen
in the latter: coal contains only about half the amount
found in petroleum. Therefore, conversion of coal into
liquid fuels involves the addition of hydrogen.

LIQUEFACTION REACTIONS

Hydrogenation of coal can be done directly, either from
gaseous hydrogen or by a liquid hydrogen-donor solvent,

or it can be done indirectly, through an intermediate series of compounds. In direct liquefaction, the macromolecular structure of the coal is broken down in such a manner that the yield of the correct size of molecules is maximized and the production of the very small molecules that constitute fuel gases is minimized. By contrast, indirect liquefaction methods break down the coal structure all the way to a synthesis gas mixture (carbon monoxide and hydrogen), and these molecules are used to rebuild the desired liquid hydrocarbon molecules.

Since coal is a complex substance, it is often represented in chemical symbols by an average composition. Given this simplification, direct liquefaction can be illustrated as follows:

$$CH_{0.8}S_{0.2}O_{0.1}N_{0.01} + H_2 \longrightarrow (RCH_x) + CO_2, H_2S, NH_3, H_2O.$$

Direct liquefaction of coal can be achieved with and without catalysts (represented by R), using high pressures (200 to 700 atmospheres) and temperatures ranging between 425° and 480° C (800° and 900° F).

In the indirect liquefaction process, coal is first gasified to produce synthesis gas and then converted to liquid fuels:

$$CH_{0.8}S_{0.2}O_{0.1}N_{0.01} \longrightarrow CO + H_2 + H_2S, NH_3, H_2O$$
(gasification)
$$CO + 2H_2 \longrightarrow CH_3OH \text{ (methanol synthesis)}$$
$$2CH_3OH \longrightarrow CH_3OCH_3 + H_2O \text{ (methanol to gasoline)}$$
$$nCO + 2nH_2 \longrightarrow (-CH_2-)_n + H_2O$$
(Fischer-Tropsch synthesis)
$$nCO + (2n + 1)H_2 \longrightarrow (-CH_2-)_{n+1} + H_2O.$$

The principal variables that affect the yield and distribution of products in direct liquefaction are the solvent properties (such as stability and hydrogen-transfer capability), coal rank and maceral composition, reaction conditions, and the presence or absence of catalytic effects. Although most coals (except anthracites) can be converted into liquid products, bituminous coals are the most suitable feedstock for direct liquefaction since they produce the highest yields of desirable liquids. Medium-rank coals are the most reactive under liquefaction conditions. Among the various petrographic components, the sum of the vitrinite and liptinite maceral contents correlates well with the total yield of liquid products.

LIQUEFACTION PROCESSES

The chemical reactions outlined above are applied in specific processes, the most important of which had their origin in the first half of the 20th century.

THE BERGIUS PROCESS

The first commercially available liquefaction process was the Bergius process, developed in Germany during World War I. This involves dissolving coal in a recycled solvent oil and reacting with hydrogen under high pressures ranging from 200 to 700 atmospheres. An iron oxide catalyst is also employed. Temperatures in the reactor are in the range of 425–480 °C (800–900 °F). Light and heavy liquid fractions are separated from the ash to produce gasoline and recycle oil, respectively. In general, one ton of coal produces about 150 to 170 litres (40 to 44 gallons) of gasoline, 190 litres (50 gallons) of diesel fuel, and 130 litres (34 gallons) of fuel oil. The separation of ash and heavy liquids, along with erosion from cyclic pressurization, pose difficulties that have caused this process to be kept out of use since World War II.

The Fischer-Tropsch Process

In the first-generation, indirect liquefaction process called Fischer-Tropsch synthesis, coal is gasified first in a high-pressure Lurgi gasifier, and the resulting synthesis gas is reacted over an iron-based catalyst either in a fixed-bed or fluidized-bed reactor. Depending on reaction conditions, the products obtained consist of a wide range of hydrocarbons. Although this process was developed and used widely in Germany during World War II, it was discontinued afterward owing to poor economics. It has been in operation since the early 1950s in South Africa (the SASOL process) and now supplies as much as one-third of that country's liquid fuels.

ADVANCED PROCESSES

Lower operating temperatures are desirable in direct liquefaction processes, since higher temperatures tend to promote cracking of molecules and produce more gaseous and solid products at the expense of liquids. Similarly, lower pressures are desirable for ease and cost of operation. Research efforts in the areas of direct liquefaction have concentrated on reducing the operating pressure, improving the separation process by using a hydrogen donor solvent, operating without catalysts, and using a solvent without catalysts but using external catalytic rehydrogenation of the solvent. Research has also focused on multistage liquefaction in an effort to minimize hydrogen consumption and maximize overall process yields.

In the area of indirect liquefaction, later versions of the SASOL process have employed only fluidized-bed reactors in order to increase the yield of gasoline and have reacted excess methane with steam in order to produce more carbon monoxide and hydrogen. Other developments include producing liquid fuels from synthesis gas through an intermediate step of converting the gas into methanol at relatively low operating pressures (5 to 10 atmospheres) and temperatures (205–300 °C, or

400–575 °F). The methanol is then converted into a range of liquid hydrocarbons. The use of zeolite catalysts has enabled the direct production of gasoline from methanol with high efficiency.

CONCLUSION

Coal, petroleum, and natural gas are fossil fuels—materials of biological origin occurring within Earth's crust that can be used as a source of energy. All contain carbon and were formed as a result of geologic processes acting on the remains of organic matter produced by photosynthesis, a process that began in the Archean Eon more than 3 billion years ago. Most carbonaceous material occurring before the Devonian Period (approximately 415 million years ago) was derived from algae and bacteria.

All fossil fuels can be burned in air or with oxygen derived from air to provide heat. This heat may be employed directly, as in the case of home furnaces, or utilized to produce steam to drive generators that can supply electricity. In still other cases—for example, gas turbines used in jet aircraft—the heat yielded by burning a fossil fuel serves to increase both the pressure and the temperature of the combustion products to furnish motive power.

Since the late 18th century, fossil fuels have been consumed at an ever-increasing rate. Today they supply nearly 90 percent of all the energy consumed by the industrially developed countries of the world. The amounts of fossil fuels that can be recovered economically are difficult to estimate, largely because of changing rates of consumption and future value as well as technological developments. However, one fact is undeniable. Although new deposits of petroleum and coal continue to be discovered, the reserves of the principal fossil fuels remaining in the Earth are fixed in quantity and cannot be renewed.

anthracite The most highly metamorphosed form of coal.

bitumen Any of various solid or semisolid mixtures of hydrocarbons that occur in nature or that are obtained as residues from the distillation of petroleum or coal.

catalytic Pertaining to a modification, especially an increase in the rate of a chemical reaction, induced by material unchanged chemically at the end of the reaction.

colloidal Refers to a substance that consists of particles dispersed throughout another substance; the particles are very small but still incapable of passing through a semipermeable membrane.

conodont fossils Minute, toothlike fossils composed of the mineral apatite (calcium phosphate), most frequently occurring in marine sedimentary rocks of Paleozoic age.

diagenesis The sum of all processes, chiefly chemical, by which changes in a sediment are brought about after its deposition but before its final conversion to rock.

distillates Liquid products condensed from vapour during the distillation process.

hydrocarbons Any of a class of organic chemical compounds composed only of the elements carbon and hydrogen.

igneous Used to describe a variety of rocks made up of hardened lava, or created as the result of other volcanic activity.

kerogen The dark-coloured, insoluble product of bacterially altered plant and animal detritus; the first stage of petroleum.

lignites A type of coal, generally yellow to dark brown in color, which forms from peat at shallow depths and temperatures lower than 100 °C (212 °F).

macerals The many microscopically recognizable, individual organic constituents of coal that retain certain characteristic physical and chemical properties.

naphtha Volatile, highly flammable liquid hydrocarbon mixtures used chiefly as solvents and diluents, as well as raw materials for conversion to gasoline.

sapropelic coal A hydrogen-rich form of coal that is derived from loose deposits of sedimentary rock rich in hydrocarbons.

sedimentary Used to describe a type of rock that formed at or near Earth's surface due to the accumulation and lithification of sediment, or by the precipitation from solution at normal surface temperatures (chemical rock).

siliceous Being composed primarily of silica or a silicate.

slurry A watery mixture or suspension of insoluble matter; pulverized coal mixed with water is a slurry that can be used as fuel.

smelting The process by which a metal is obtained from its ore by heating beyond the melting point in the presence of oxidizing agents, such as air, or reducing agents, such as coke.

viscosity The property of resistance to flow in a fluid or semifluid.

BIBLIOGRAPHY

PETROLEUM

B.P. Tissot and D.H. Welte, *Petroleum Formation and Occurrence*, 2nd rev. ed. (1984); and John M. Hunt, *Petroleum Geochemistry and Geology*, 2nd ed. (1996), are sources of information on theories of the origin and accumulation of petroleum, as well as on the practical applications of scientific knowledge to petroleum problems. Marlan W. Downey, William A. Morgan, and Jack C. Threet (eds.), *Petroleum Provinces of the Twenty-First Century* (2001), is a collection of essays on such topics as the importance of oil-field discoveries of the 1990s and the availability of fossil fuels in the 21st century. Michel T. Halbouty (ed.), *Giant Oil and Gas Fields of the Decade, 1990–1999* (2003), contains lists and descriptions of the world's giant oil and gas fields.

Each year maps, production figures, and geologic data are published by *World Oil* and the *Oil and Gas Journal*.

PETROLEUM PRODUCTION

Two books that explain the entire petroleum process in laypersons' terms, from formation to prospecting to drilling and recovery, are Norman J. Hyne, *Nontechnical Guide to Petroleum Geology, Exploration, Drilling and Production*, 2nd ed. (2001), by a professor of petroleum geology; and Martin Raymond and William L. Leffler, *Oil and Gas Production in Nontechnical Language* (2006), by an industry veteran and a technical writer. William C. Lyons and Gary

J. Plisga, *Standard Handbook of Petroleum and Natural Gas Engineering*, 2nd ed. (2005), is a technical reference work.

PETROLEUM REFINING

Bill D. Berger and Kenneth E. Anderson, *Modern Petroleum: A Basic Primer of the Industry*, 3rd ed. (1992), is a nontechnical introduction to the entire petroleum industry that provides a good understanding of the interaction between exploration, drilling, transportation, refining, petrochemicals, and marketing. A simple introduction to petroleum refinery processes is William L. Leffler, *Petroleum Refining in Nontechnical Language*, 4th ed. (2008), with chapters on each major process. More detailed descriptions of processes and typical operating considerations are provided in Robert A. Meyers (ed.), *Handbook of Petroleum Refining Processes*, 3rd ed. (2004); and James G. Speight, *The Chemistry and Technology of Petroleum*, 4th ed. (2007).

NATURAL GAS

Arlon R. Tussing and Connie C. Barlow, *The Natural Gas Industry* (1984), provides a history of the industry in the United States beginning with coal gasification in the 19th century through the development of government regulatory programs in the 1980s; in addition, the structural evolution of the domestic gas industry is described, with special emphasis on the impact of industry regulations. R.V. Smith, *Practical Natural Gas Engineering*, 2nd ed. (1990), discusses technical aspects of gas production.

COAL

G.H. Taylor et al., *Organic Petrology* (1998); BP/Amoco, *BP Statistical Review of World Energy* (2006); and the World

Energy Council, *Survey of Energy Resources* (2004), provide data on proven reserves.

Simon Walker, *Major Coalfields of the World* (2000), provides information about coal resources worldwide. Information on the organic composition of coals, with numerous references to earlier literature, may be found in D.W. van Krevelen, *Coal: Typology, Physics, Chemistry, Constitution*, 3rd, completely rev. ed. (1993). Douglas C. Peters (ed.), *Geology in Coal Resource Utilization* (1991), provides information concerning coal resources, reserve estimation, coal utilization, and the environment.

COAL MINING

Kristina Lindbergh and Barry Provorse, *Coal—A Contemporary Energy Story*, rev. ed. (1980), provides nontechnical information on coal geology, mining, transportation, and utilization. Roy D. Merritt, *Coal Exploration, Mine Planning, and Development* (1986), offers details on geology and exploration. All aspects of mining engineering, including coal mining, are discussed in Howard L. Hartman, *Introductory Mining Engineering*, 2nd ed. (2002); Howard L. Hartman (ed.), *SME Mining Engineering Handbook*, 2nd ed., 2 vol. (1992); and Bruce A. Kennedy (ed.), *Surface Mining*, 2nd ed. (1990). Robert Stefanko, *Coal Mining Technology: Theory and Practice* (1983), is a standard reference for underground coal-mine operating practices in the United States.

COAL UTILIZATION

Harold H. Schobert, *Coal, the Energy Source of the Past and the Future* (1987), provides a good nontechnical introduction to coal for a reader with little or no chemical background; it also provides an understanding of the role that coal has played in society from ancient times to the present. N. Berkowitz, *An Introduction to Coal Technology*, 2nd ed. (1993), is useful for a reader learning about coal for the first time. James G. Speight, *The Chemistry and Technology of Coal*, 2nd ed., revised and expanded (1994), an introductory textbook, deals with geology, petrography, chemistry, and utilization technology. D. Merrick, *Coal Combustion and Conversion Technology* (1984), offers a comprehensive guide to coal-utilization technology for engineers, planners, and policy makers. Other books are H.-D. Schilling, B. Bonn, and U. Krauss, *Coal Gasification: Existing Processes and New Developments*, 2nd rev. ed. (1981; originally published in German, 2nd rev. ed., 1979), a comprehensive collection; and Perry Nowacki, *Coal Liquefaction Processes* (1979), a systematic discussion.

INDEX